Your Second Wedding

HOW TO HANDLE ISSUES, MAKE PLANS, AND ENSURE IT'S A GREAT SUCCESS

By Kristie Lorette

Your Second Wedding: How to Handle Issues, Make Plans, and Ensure it's a Great Success

Library of Congress Cataloging-in-Publication Data

Lorette, Kristie, 1975-
  Your second wedding : how to handle issues, make plans, and ensure it's a great success / Kristie Lorette.
     p. cm.
  Includes bibliographical references and index.
  ISBN 978-1-60138-629-8 (alk. paper) -- ISBN 1-60138-629-X (alk. paper) 1. Weddings--Planning. 2. Wedding etiquette. 3. Remarriage. I. Title.
  HQ745.L675 2012
  306.84--dc23
                              2012015621

Printed in the United States
PROJECT MANAGER: Crystal Edwards • cedwards@atlantic-pub.com
PROOFREADING: C&P Marse • bluemoon6749@bellsouth.net
BOOK PRODUCTION DESIGN: T.L. Price • design@tlpricefreelance.com
FRONT/BACK COVER DESIGN: Jackie Miller • millerjackiej@gmail.com

Printed on Recycled Paper

A few years back we lost our beloved pet dog Bear, who was not only our best and dearest friend but also the "Vice President of Sunshine" here at Atlantic Publishing. He did not receive a salary but worked tirelessly 24 hours a day to please his parents.

Bear was a rescue dog who turned around and showered myself, my wife, Sherri, his grandparents Jean, Bob, and Nancy, and every person and animal he met (well, maybe not rabbits) with friendship and love. He made a lot of people smile every day.

We wanted you to know a portion of the profits of this book will be donated in Bear's memory to local animal shelters, parks, conservation organizations, and other individuals and nonprofit organizations in need of assistance.

– *Douglas & Sherri Brown*

PS: We have since adopted two more rescue dogs: first Scout, and the following year, Ginger. They were both mixed golden retrievers who needed a home.

Want to help animals and the world? Here are a dozen easy suggestions you and your family can implement today:

- *Adopt and rescue a pet from a local shelter.*
- *Support local and no-kill animal shelters.*
- *Plant a tree to honor someone you love.*
- *Be a developer — put up some birdhouses.*
- *Buy live, potted Christmas trees and replant them.*
- *Make sure you spend time with your animals each day.*
- *Save natural resources by recycling and buying recycled products.*
- *Drink tap water, or filter your own water at home.*
- *Whenever possible, limit your use of or do not use pesticides.*
- *If you eat seafood, make sustainable choices.*
- *Support your local farmers market.*
- *Get outside. Visit a park, volunteer, walk your dog, or ride your bike.*

Five years ago, Atlantic Publishing signed the Green Press Initiative. These guidelines promote environmentally friendly practices, such as using recycled stock and vegetable-based inks, avoiding waste, choosing energy-efficient resources, and promoting a no-pulping policy. We now use 100-percent recycled stock on all our books. The results: in one year, switching to post-consumer recycled stock saved 24 mature trees, 5,000 gallons of water, the equivalent of the total energy used for one home in a year, and the equivalent of the greenhouse gases from one car driven for a year.

Table of Contents

Chapter 3: Types of Second Weddings 39

Chapter 4: Get Organized — Plan for the Planning 51

Chapter 5: The Bridal Party 71

Chapter 6: Legal Requirements for a Second Marriage 95

Chapter 7: Saying I Do 103

Chapter 8: The Celebration 123

Chapter 9: Invitations and Wedding Stationery 137

Chapter 10: The Blooms 151

Chapter 11: Let Us Entertain Them.........169

Chapter 12: You Ought to Be in Pictures ..183

Chapter 13: Let Them Eat Cake 201

Chapter 14: What to Wear 213

Chapter 15: Getting To and Fro 241

Chapter 16: Other Wedding Celebrations 249

Chapter 17: Gift Registry 269

Introduction

Congratulations on getting engaged and planning your wedding! Welcome to the ranks of those planning their second wedding — or maybe even their third, fourth, fifth, or eighth wedding, Elizabeth Taylor style. The great thing about planning a wedding is that each event is its own event, which means that no two weddings are ever alike. Whether this is your first time getting married, but your spouse-to-be is doing it for the second time around, or it is a  second time for both of you, this wedding should reflect your personalities, your relationship, and your love.

Although the majority of first timers do not enter into the union of marriage with the plan to get a divorce, it happens. When a couple is planning their wedding, no one imagines a time when he or she will not be with the person standing next to him or her at the altar. However, statistics show that this is not always the case. According to **www.divorceguide.com**, 50 percent of American first marriages end in divorce and 65 percent of second marriages end in divorce. And, divorce is not always the culprit. You also could have found your second true love after the death of your first wife or husband early in your married life. If you are a widow or widower, marrying the second love of your life can be more emotional because the loss of a spouse is different than when you divorce. Some people feel a sense of guilt or betrayal toward their first spouses, even though the spouses are gone, because they took their vows for life and death. What you have to learn is how to allow yourself to move on and have the happiness you deserve and that your first spouse would want you to enjoy.

If your first marriage ended in divorce, then you ideally have learned lessons on what does and what does not work in a marriage. You are also a different person now than you were the first time around. You might be older and wiser now, or you might know yourself better than you did when you chose your first spouse. All of these lessons and changes in life alter who you are as a person and whom you choose to spend the rest of your life with. Take the lessons you have learned from your first marriage and apply them to making your second marriage even better. Even if you are a widow or a widower, you can draw from the experiences of your first marriage to ensure your second marriage is just as happy, or even happier, than your first marriage. The primary thing to keep in mind is that each relationship is different, and you need to enter into your second marriage treating it as its own separate entity.

Planning a second wedding produces a lot of anxiety for the bride and groom. Planning a wedding is stressful, period. When you add that there might be children and exes involved in the process, the stress levels increase. Some second brides and grooms even might feel guilty about getting a second chance at happiness.

As a former certified event planner, I have watched both first-time and second-time brides go through the process of planning their weddings. I have provided advice and guidance to many of the people involved — the bride, the groom, the parents, the bridal party, and more. The most important advice I can give is included in this book, and it is not just my opinion either. It is the advice I have compiled from what I have learned from my experiences working with couples just like you — those embarking on a new marriage as an encore bride or groom. It is also the advice of other wedding professionals that work in the industry, and even brides and grooms that have gone down the aisle a second time before you, paving the way for your second wedding to be the best one yet.

How This Book Can Help

This book is a comprehensive guide to planning a second wedding. Although many aspects of a second wedding are different from those of a first wedding, others are the same. The primary focus of this book is to help you deal specifically with the aspects of planning a second wedding, but it also includes helpful advice for every part of planning a wedding — first one, second, third one, or beyond.

You will learn how to approach the planning process for your second wedding, such as dealing with your feelings about your first wedding, telling your children, your ex, and your ex-family members you are tying the knot again. In addition, you will uncover the different styles of weddings you can opt for in a second wedding and then get into the details of planning both the wedding ceremony and the reception. You also will discover some of the etiquette and feelings about planning a second wedding versus a first wedding and how to overcome each of these issues. You will find practical advice on budgeting, choosing venues, saving money, and tips, tricks, advice from professional wedding planners and other professionals in the industry. You even will find advice from those second brides and grooms that have gone down the aisle before you. This book includes checklists, planning worksheets, and sample ideas to help you get and stay organized throughout the planning process.

Before you get into the details of planning your wedding and putting together your second chance at love, keep one thing in mind. The only thing that really matters is you and your significant other, the person marrying you. If you both show up at the ceremony and exchange your vows, it was a success. Even if everything does not go exactly as planned, the reason for the wedding is to join the two of you as one. If the flowers do not turn out exactly the way you wanted them or the cake is melting a little, it really does not matter because it is not what the true meaning of the wedding is really about. Although some things will go off without a hitch, it is inevitable that some problem will pop up during the ceremony or reception. Just take a deep breath, breathe in and out, and let it go. It does not matter as long as you are happy and are together. In fact, laughing about it makes light of the situation and does not allow the mishap to turn into a major dilemma that destroys your wedding day.

Now that you have the right perspective, it is time to get started. So, roll up your sleeves, put on your thinking cap, and let's start working on planning your second wedding.

The Difference Between the First and Second I Dos

Think back for just a moment about the person you were when you were planning your walk down the aisle for the first time. Do not dwell on it too long, but now think about the person you are today. You have changed and evolved over the years and from the experiences you have had in between marriages. This chapter covers the differences in planning a wedding when it is the second wedding for the groom, but not the bride; a second wedding for the bride but not the groom; and when it is a second wedding for both.

For example, it is tradition for the bride's parents to pay for the wedding. If it is the bride's second wedding, however, it is more common for the bride and groom to pay for it themselves. The chapter also talks about the typical etiquette rules of a second wedding. But do not let traditions get in your way if you have other ideas for your special day. Many brides and grooms are shunning these rules and doing it their way from the start of their new lives together. As another example, a common debate among previously married new couples is whether they should register for gifts or have a **bridal shower**. After all, these wedding celebrations are to help the bride and groom set up their first home. In a second wedding situation, the couple already might have typical household items, so they might choose not to register or have a bridal shower, or choose alternatives to the traditional gift registry.

When One of You Has Been Married Before but the Other Has Not

 Getting swept up in the euphoria of planning a wedding can be an exciting time in a couple's life. Again, it is all about how you approach getting married the second time. If one of you has been down the aisle before, it can be a little less euphoric because it is not a new experience, but it is a different experience. The previously married person's outlook might be different from the point of view he or she had planning the first wedding. A common example is when one partner has been married before, but it is the other's first time. Let's say the man has been married, but the woman has not. In a scenario such as this, the bride might want her big dream wedding, while the groom would prefer to have a small, intimate affair because he had a big fancy wedding the first time around. Or you might get lucky, and you both might want the style of wedding a certain way. *The styles of weddings will be discussed in Chapter 3.*

Communication between you and your spouse-to-be is imperative. Each of you probably has your own thoughts on how the ceremony and reception should be, and until you have a conversation about your ideas for the wedding, you cannot proceed with the decisions that need to be made in order to start the planning process.

One of the primary things to keep in mind when discussing these decisions with your partner is to not compare your first wedding with your second wedding. Each event is its own entity. This rule applies to both of you, whether you are the one that has been married before or not. The second wedding ceremony and reception is not to outdo the first wedding, to

get it up to par with the first wedding, or to compete in any way, shape, or form. It is vital to treat your wedding as its own event and proceed with the planning process that way.

Comparing the first wedding with what is happening with the second wedding can cause fighting and strife. Although you should share your honest feelings with your future spouse, it is also wise to pick your battles. If your spouse-to-be continuously is saying, "That's not what we did when I got married the first time," calmly express your understanding of what he or she is saying, but explain that it is important to you that you plan this wedding as its own event, rather than similar to, different to, or in competition with the first wedding.

Only you have the ability to draw the line between the first and second weddings. Yes, you can take your experience in planning your first wedding and apply it to the second wedding. Yes, you can listen to the advice your mom, friends, and bridesmaids give, even if it is similar to the advice some of them gave for the first wedding. In the end, however, it is you, and you alone, who has to live with the decisions you make. It is fine to let your mind wander back to the first wedding, but avoid dwelling on it to the point where it interferes with your feelings, emotions, and planning of the second wedding. In the end, it is all about your mindset. You have to separate the two events in your own mind. Once you do this, you can pull ideas from your first wedding, uncover new ideas for your second wedding, and not even think about the fact that you are using the same caterer — just that you are using a magnificent caterer.

In other words, you have to learn how to trust another person again, just as you did your first spouse. Open communication about the situation helps you and your spouse-to-be get everything out on the table and work through any problems or issues before they turn into arguments and resentment.

When You Have Both Been Married Before

In the majority of cases, when it is a second wedding for both partners, they tend to be more focused on the meaning of the wedding rather than the type of celebration. In fact, the meaning of the ceremony should be the focal point no matter how many times each of you has been married before.

Therefore, because the couple wants to remember why they are there instead of getting caught up in extravagant planning, it is less likely that a second wedding for both the bride and the groom is a big, grand affair. Typically, it tends to be a small, intimate affair. In fact, many second weddings are made up of the couple, the **officiant** or person performing the wedding ceremony, and a couple of witnesses. If one or more of you has children or parents who are still living, these special people are also included. However, as has been mentioned several times, this is your special day. Plan, organize, and party as much or as little as *you* want.

The Rule Is There Are No Rules

Although etiquette often declares what is and is not proper for a second wedding, the modern bride and groom are making up their own rules. Again, these decisions all come back to the preferences of the bride and groom. Should a bride getting married for the second time who has two children from her previous marriage wear a white wedding gown? The modern second wedding couple says, "Sure, why not?"

Etiquette is a guide and not a rule book. Some people feel they have to do everything by the book; you might feel the need to follow the etiquette on a second marriage, dotting all of your I's and crossing all of your T's. If following etiquette is not important to you, then the good news is that there is not an etiquette police department that will cite you for making a decision about your second wedding that is not in line with the guidelines.

On the other hand, you will have many friends and family members who have their own opinions on what you should and should not do. For example, friends and family members that were guests at your first wedding might have chosen an expensive household item from your registry. Because the second wedding involves the merging of two more complete households than a first wedding, these friends and family members might not feel inclined to spend money on another expensive gift.

Although certain actions might offend family and friends, such as wearing a white dress, a gift registry, or asking parents to pay for a big wedding, in the end, the *couple* should decide what they do and do not want. It is fair, however, to consider these opinions when making your own decisions.

You can read through book after book, including this book, to find out all the details you need to know to plan your second wedding, but in the end, what you decide should express your personality, your likes and dislikes, and what makes you comfortable. In essence, you can throw the rule book right out of the window and plan the wedding you want, the way you want it.

As you and your spouse-to-be communicate and get on the same page, it is then time to start incorporating everybody else into your plan. Just as you want to do with any major event in your life, one of the first things to do when you get engaged is to call all of your family and friends, show off your ideas for invitations to all your coworkers, even call in at your local radio station to express your newfound happiness. However, when you are dealing with a second wedding, matters tend to be a little bit more delicate. *Chapter 2 covers how to share the big news that still allows you to get the word out, but in the right order and without stepping on anyone's toes or hurting anyone's feelings.*

CHAPTER TWO

Making the Big Announcement

Getting engaged is an exciting time in your life. While the first time you get engaged is a new experience, the second time around is just as exciting and emotional and is still a new experience. Emotions run high when you get engaged. You and your fiancé are excited and cannot wait to scream from the mountaintops that you are in love, engaged, and heading off to the chapel (or some other venue) to get married. However, although your engagement and impending marriage are exciting, happy events for you and your fiancé, the emotions running through the rest of your family might be on the other end of the spectrum.

This chapter has tips and advice on how to go about announcing your engagement so that you can share the exciting news with your loved ones but not hurt others in the process. Remember, when you are a second-time bride or groom, there are often ex-spouses, children, and even ex in-laws involved. This chapter uncovers the options for telling the children from each previous relationship and dealing with the emotions the children might have about combining the families. Finally, the chapter covers how to tell your ex-spouses and your ex-in-laws (if necessary), as well as how to send out formal announcements to all your friends.

Telling Your Children

If one or both of you have children from your previous marriage or relationship, the children should be the first to know, before you tell anyone else. Even if your children get along great with your boyfriend or girlfriend, your children's emotions are going to change when you tell them you are getting married. Whether the children's other parent is divorced or deceased, the children tend to want their parents to be together. It can be a difficult situation to introduce someone as a parental figure into their lives. Even if their biological parent will remain in their lives, your new spouse plays a vital role in their futures. It is important to approach the situation of telling the children in a sensitive and delicate manner, and they should find out this news from you, their parent, before they find out from someone else.

Mom and dad should tell their respective children alone

If you are the bride-to-be, sit down alone with your children to have the discussion. Let them know how much you love them and how they always will be the most important thing in your life. Then you will want to talk a little bit about the relationship you have with your fiancé. You also should engage the children in the conversation by asking about how they feel about him. Once you open up the two-way communication, let the kids know how much you love your fiancé and that he is going to become your new husband and their new stepfather.

Reassure your children that your new husband is not going to replace their father. If their father is still alive and involved in their lives, then let the children know the relationship they have with their dad will not change. Explain to them that by your new husband coming into your family, they will have even more people that love and care about them. So, now instead of just having a mom and dad who love them, they have a stepfather, or whatever title you want to give your new husband, who loves them too.

If you are on good terms with your ex-husband, you might want to talk with him about the engagement first. This allows you to both be there for the children when you make the announcement. This shows your children a united front between you  and their father and shows their father's support of your entering into this new relationship and forming this new family. This can be helpful in easing the transition for the children, so they do not feel as if they are betraying their father by having a relationship with your spouse-to-be.

After you have made the announcement to the children, ask them how they feel. Find out if they have any questions about how things might change after the marriage. Prepare yourself because your children might have questions that surprise you or set you back for a moment, such as: Do they have to listen to what your new husband tells them to do and will their father still be involved in their lives? If they ask you a question that you cannot immediately answer, tell them you will think about it and get back to them later. Just make sure you revisit the question as soon as possible and provide the children with the best answer you can.

When you share your big and exciting news with your children, they might not find it so exciting. Some kids might get angry, while others might be so upset they burst into tears. In the ideal situation, the kids are happy and adjust quickly, and everyone moves on in planning the wedding. However, anger and sadness are valid emotions for your children to feel, and you should address these feelings with the children. Start by asking the child why he or she is mad or crying. Try to get to unhappy children to explain to you in their own words what is causing them to feel the emotions they are having.

When the child tells you how he or she is feeling, validate those feelings. Say that you understand how he or she feels. Repeat back your understanding of his or her emotions. Then, talk with your children about how you plan to work through each of their concerns. For example, a child might cry because he thinks he will not see his real father anymore. In this situation, explain that his father is always going to be his father. Reassure him that the visitation schedule he has with his father is not changing, that he will simply have a stepfather who will love and care about him, too.

If you are the groom-to-be, tell your children about your impending marriage on your own as well. Follow the same steps that the bride-to-be follows in announcing the big news, and answer any questions your children might have. If you have a good relationship with your ex-wife and the mother of the kids, you might want to tell her first, and then the both of you can tell the children together. It is affirmation for the children that it is acceptable to their mother, who can help the children accept the new relationship and marriage faster and is easier than trying to convince the kids on your own.

CASE STUDY: TELLING ALL THE CHILDREN TOGETHER

Charles and Linda Van Kessler
204 N. El Camino Real, Suite E-736
Encinitas, CA 92024
760-518-2780
linda@passion4lifevitamins.com
www.passion4lifevitamins.com;
www.passionkids.org

When Charles and Linda Van Kessler decided to marry for the second time, Linda was a widow and Charles was divorced. In Linda's first wedding, she was married at the groom's home because she is Christian and her first husband was Jewish, which prevented them from marrying in a church or a synagogue.

Charles, the second husband-to-be, proposed to Linda at the family Christmas celebration, which included Linda and Charles, as well as their children from their first marriages. The last gift given out was to Linda from Charles and was an engagement ring.

Linda and Charles chose to tell their children about the engagement and impending marriage together. They chose to do it this way because they wanted the children to share in the excitement of the moment and see their happiness, which was infectious. They both wanted them to know that the engagement/marriage was an intertwining the two families forever. They wanted the kids to feel the excitement of "knowing a secret" no one else knew; Charles and Linda did not want anyone else to hear the news before the children. Their children were thrilled for the couple and did not have any negative reactions.

The children's involvement did not end with the engagement either. The only wedding party included was the couple's three children. Charles's son was his best man, his daughter was Linda's maid of honor, and Linda's son was the groomsman. They wanted their children to be part of the ceremony, as their families were joining, so they knew this marriage included them. They did not want them to feel like their mom or dad was now going to be out of their lives or have less time for them, or that this new life would not include them. Charles and Linda wanted the children to know nothing had changed in their relationships with them except that now their family was complete with a mom and dad and new brothers and sisters.

Group meeting

Once each of you has told your own children, plan a time when both families come together and have a big group discussion. The discussion should include the process of combining two families into one big family.

Some of the discussion topics might include:

- Where you will live. If you are the primary caregiver to your children, or your spouse is, then explain that the only thing that will change is that there will be more of you living in one house. If you plan to buy or rent a new home to accommodate your growing family, then share this information with your kids as well.

- What the rules of the new house will be. Primarily, the rules of the new house entail how the new residents will all live together in harmony. First, this means that your new spouse, as an adult, is one of the new "bosses" of the house, which means that the children have to listen and obey what he or she says. Rules about living with and interacting with their new siblings are also important to establish so the children can begin to adhere to them as soon as possible.

- How the roles of the children might change. Because new children might be joining the household, this means that chores and roles might shift slightly. Instead of one child being responsible for handling the laundry, a laundry buddy might be assigned to handle the new volume of clothing.

- Bedroom situations. Again, if more children are coming into the home, then children of the same sex might have to double or triple up in rooms to accommodate everyone. Older children, or children that do not have siblings of the same sex, might be able to keep their own rooms.

- How you want to include the children in the planning, ceremony, and reception of the wedding. Telling the children that they will play a big role in the wedding can add the excitement required to get them over some of the angst they might be feeling. During the family discussion, you want to stress how the marriage is not just about you and your fiancé but is about them, too. *Chapter 5 will discuss ways to make your children a part of your special day.*

Telling the Ex-Spouse

Telling your ex and his or her family can be a difficult process. It all depends on the relationship you have with them. Keep in mind that the way you tell your ex and his or her parents is also to focus on perpetuating the good relationship your children have with this side of their family.

In reality, telling your ex and his or her family has nothing to do with you; it is all about what is in the best interest of the children. Sit down face-to-face with your ex, if possible, to share the news. Do it alone and not in front of the children. As far as your ex in-laws are concerned, you can opt to call them or see them face-to-face with the news. Between you and your ex-spouse, you also might decide the news is better coming from him or her rather than you. Again, these are personal decisions that really come down to the type of relationship you have with your ex-spouse and the kind of relationship you have with your ex in-laws.

If you do not have children, it is up to you whether you share the news with your ex and his or her family. If you and your ex have maintained a friendship after your marriage ended, and  your spouse-to-be does not have a problem with you sharing the news, feel free to give him or her a call or meet in person to let him or her know. On the other hand, if you have not maintained a relationship with your ex and you do not have any children with him or her, you do not have an obligation to let him or her know you are remarrying.

If you are lucky, your ex will understand and be happy you have found a new love. The other side of the coin is an ex-spouse who becomes angry or antagonistic. If you are a woman telling her ex-husband she is marrying her new boyfriend, and if your ex becomes irate, remain calm. Try calming him down by telling him that you are not yelling, and therefore, he should not be yelling either. Assure him you want to talk about it, and remind him that the focus is the children you have together. Remind your ex that you do not have to be best friends, and you do not need his permission to remarry, but that co-parenting is the most important thing both of you have to focus on. You need his cooperation to accomplish this.

Not every ex-spouse is going to calm down and agree to everything you say. It might take time for him or her to warm up to the idea. Simply keep reminding him or her what the important thing is — the children. When you add logic to the equation, it helps to calm the emotional side of the news and redirect the anger or emotional side to a logistical issue.

Making the Public Announcement

One of the traditional steps in announcing the big news in a first wedding is to place an engagement announcement in the newspaper. For a second wedding, it is less of a traditional move to take, but it is not a prohibited one. If you want to place  an engagement announcement in the newspaper, then feel free to do so. If you are trying to keep as close to etiquette as possible, you might want to skip the newspaper announcement.

Once you have made the announcement to your children and your ex, move on to telling your close family. Traditionally, a man goes to the bride's father to ask for her hand in marriage. If it is the first wedding for the bride, this is a tradition you might want to adhere to. If your groom-to-be wishes to ask for the bride's hand in marriage, this is an occasion when the parents of the bride know about the impending marriage before the kids do. A marriage proposal is a question that should be asked in a face-to-face situation whenever possible.

For other members of the family, a phone call or email is adequate in announcing the engagement. If it is a first marriage for one of you, you might wish to send out formal engagement announcements. Even in a first wedding situation, sending out formal engagement announcements is a preference rather than a necessity.

After you announce the big day, it is now time to start getting into the planning process. Before you can truly dive into planning all of the minute details, you have to start with the first step, which is to choose the style of wedding you wish to have. *Chapter 3 discusses the details of choosing the style of wedding you and your spouse-to-be want to have.*

CHAPTER THREE

Types of Second Weddings

Are you thinking about what your Great Aunt Sally will say if you dare walk down the aisle for the second time wearing a white dress? What about your grandmother and her opinions on whether you should have the big bash you had the first time around? As is the case in a first wedding, you as a couple can choose from various wedding styles to plan a second wedding. The style depends on your own personal tastes. Preferences and tastes can be influenced by whether one or both of you previously have been married. A second wedding can include a traditional church and reception wedding, destination wedding, a civil ceremony at the courthouse, or an intimate affair. An intimate affair might consist only of the bride, groom, officiant, and a few people special to the bride and groom.

Traditional

The most common type of first or second wedding for most couples is a traditional wedding. A traditional wedding is typically a formal affair with all of the bells, whistles, and customs included in the wedding ceremony and wedding reception. Traditional wedding ceremonies tend to be religious ceremonies, so they take place in a church, synagogue, or other religious institution. Regardless of if one or both parties of the couple have been married before, a traditional wedding is always an option. When one of the parties has been married before but the other one has not and the person who has not been married previously wants a big wedding, the traditional wedding most commonly is chosen.

Advantages

As is the case with any style of wedding, the traditional wedding offers advantages and disadvantages. Traditional weddings seem to be the dream wedding most brides and grooms think of when getting married. When tradition is important to one or both of you, this type of wedding fits the bill in all of the ways a wedding can.

The second primary advantage is that weddings are a rite of passage. Every rite of passage comes steeped in tradition. Choosing a traditional wedding style for a second wedding allows the couple to go through all of the routines and ceremony that makes the wedding the rite of passage it was created to be.

Disadvantages

Traditional weddings and a massive wedding budget go hand-in-hand. Because many rituals should be adhered to in order to carry out all of the traditions, traditional weddings tend to be the most expensive types of wedding styles. Another disadvantage of a traditional wedding is that it can cause complications with the ex-families. For example, putting together the guest list gets tricky with a traditional wedding. Because traditional weddings tend to be big, it does not give you an easy excuse as to why your ex-spouse and his or her parents are not on the guest list so they can be there for their children and grandchildren.

Another time traditional weddings might pose a problem is when, according to tradition, the parents of the bride pay for the wedding. If this is the second wedding for the bride, the parents of the bride might feel they have already filled their obligation the first time around, which might put a damper on the budget for the second wedding.

Although planning a wedding of any kind puts stress on the bride and groom, the traditional wedding is likely the culprit in putting the biggest amount of stress. Because of the size and the details that tend to go into planning a traditional wedding, brides and grooms tend to report the highest levels of frustration with all the details that must be perfected. This is another disadvantage of planning a traditional wedding as opposed to some of the other options available to couples. For example, a destination wedding tends to be smaller and more intimate. Destination wedding locations also tend to come with a wedding coordinator to help guide the bride and groom in making their choices. This all cuts down on the amount of stress that a bride and groom might feel when planning a traditional wedding versus a destination wedding.

CASE STUDY: TURNING OLD TRADITIONS INTO NEW TRADITIONS

Red Letter Event Planning
Robyn Bruns
2221 Pinehurst Drive
Glenview, IL 60025
773-266-0601
Robyn@RedLetterEventPlanning.com
www.RedLetterEventPlanning.com

Robyn Bruns, from Red Letter Event Planning, estimates that most of the second weddings she has worked on are a second wedding for both people. However, two of them were a second wedding for the groom and a first for the bride. Robyn says the weddings are traditional in the sense that the brides wear wedding dresses, and there is a reception. However, the guest list is usually smaller, it is in an unusual location (not a church), and there is minimal or no wedding party. In addition, the majority of second timers want it to be a good time for their guests, more like a party then a wedding reception. There are still traditional elements, such as a first dance or cake cutting, but the non-traditional elements are there as well. For example, one couple sat at one of the round tables with the immediate family from both sides, although the table did have a more elaborate centerpiece to stand out.

Robyn shares that second timers are more open to unique ideas. In her experience, second time wedding couples are not obsessed with the latest wedding trends; instead, they are looking to have a wedding that reflects who they are as a couple. For example, one couple she worked with had a reception with food stations of all Cuban food because the groom was Cuban and the bride wanted to introduce her family to her new husband's roots. Another couple wanted to have a big Italian dinner party because they both came from huge, Italian families.

Many of the traditional elements for first-time weddings are not incorporated. None of Robyn's second-time couples have been announced into the reception, none have done a bouquet or garter toss, and almost all of them stay until the last song — no formal departures with sparklers or rice throwing.

Robyn says this is an opportunity for couples to think out-of-the-box. Non-traditional elements might be to have a jazz band instead of a DJ, serve family style instead of plated, or have a brunch wedding where you serve signature mimosas and have a string quartet playing in the background. Second-time couples are more adventurous in their wedding planning, which makes the planning process a lot of fun.

The attire for the wedding is also an opportunity for the couple to be different. The second-time bride can wear a colored wedding dress and feathers in her hair and will not have to worry about a disapproving mother or grandmother. The groom can have a custom-made suit. In one of Robyn's favorite weddings, the bride wore a blue dress (not a wedding dress) and the groom wore a seersucker suit with straw hat. This is not to say they cannot wear a white dress, but most of the second time brides Robyn has worked with have put a unique spin to make their attire stand out from the dress they wore the first time.

Destination Weddings

Destination weddings have become increasingly popular over the years. These types of weddings whisk the bride and groom off to a dream spot, such as the tropics or the mountains. All-in-one resort destination **venues** tend to specialize in helping the bride and groom plan and put together these types of weddings. Destination wedding venues also tend to be a type of one-stop-shop for wedding planning, which means the bride and groom can depend on the one location to offer everything from the venue, bouquets, and officiant to the reception area, food, and entertainment. Destination weddings tend to be popular for couples that have both been married and do not want any guests or only a few guests present. Another advantage of destination weddings is the couple can have the ceremony, reception, and honeymoon all in one location.

One of the biggest advantages of hosting a destination wedding is that the one location tends to handle all of the details the bride and groom need and want for their big day. On the other hand, destination weddings can pose a disadvantage because the couple might have to travel to meet with the wedding coordinator or have to handle everything long distance. Also, they can be on the expensive side, as they involve travel, and there is no guarantee all of the desired guests will be able to afford the trip, plus accommodations, etc.

Civil Ceremonies

Civil ceremonies typically are held at the local county courthouse. A judge from the court performs the ceremony. A civil ceremony tends to include only the bride, groom, two witnesses, and the judge. A civil ceremony is also the least expensive style of wedding couples can choose. This type of ceremony is popular for couples that both have been married before and do not want any guests or only a few guests at the wedding, or do not have a lot of money to spend on the wedding.

Hands down, this is the least stressful and easiest type of wedding to plan. However, the disadvantages include not having the traditions and rituals that commonly accompany dream weddings, so this type of wedding can feel a little anticlimactic. On the other hand, it is possible to have a simple civil ceremony coupled with a larger celebration party as a follow-up.

Intimate Affairs

Intimate affairs are typically smaller weddings than traditional weddings. Intimate affairs might include all of the traditions, but the size of the wedding tends to be smaller than the typical traditional affair that could include hundreds of guests. These smaller weddings also sometimes cut out some of the traditions a typical wedding would have. Intimate wedding affairs tend to be best for couples that want a traditional wedding but have a small guest list, which allows them to share the event with their close friends and family while keeping the budget down as well.

Intimate affairs allow you to combine a couple of different elements from the other types of wedding styles, so you still get the wedding you want without going crazy or blowing your budget.

While these are the primary styles of weddings from which to choose, you also can do some mixing and matching of the styles. For example, you might opt for a civil ceremony, where it is only you, your spouse-to-be, and your two witnesses present, but then throw a huge reception, where you invite hundreds of guests to celebrate your new marriage.

Create Your Vision

It might sound a little silly at first, but go through this exercise and then have your fiancé go through it as well. After you have both completed the exercise, compare your notes and thoughts to determine which wedding style is the best one for both of you.

1. Take out a sheet of paper and or pull up a new document on your computer.
2. Close your eyes for a moment.

3. Create a descriptive vision of your wedding ceremony in your head starting with the moment you wake up that morning and prepare for the day. Think in as much detail as you possibly can.

4. Open your eyes for a moment, and record all of the details you remember.

5. Close your eyes again, and now go through the same steps for the wedding reception.

Questions to answer in creating your vision

1. Where am I getting ready for the ceremony?

2. Am I getting ready by myself, with a makeup and hair artist or with my bridal party?

3. What am I wearing?

4. What accessories am I wearing?

5. What type of venue am I at when I am walking down the aisle?

6. Who do I see in the audience as guests?

7. What decorations do I see as I walk into the ceremony location?

8. When I walk into the reception, what do I hear?

9. What kind of centerpieces are on the reception tables?

10. What is the atmosphere of the reception venue?

11. How many wedding guests do I see?

Another exercise you can use is to complete the preliminary planning worksheet below. Each of you can complete it separately and compare your answers. Or, you can go through the worksheet together and talk about each of the sections as you come to them on the worksheet.

PRELIMINARY PLANNING WORKSHEET	
Wedding Description	**Location**
❏ Formal	❏ Your home
❏ Informal	❏ Bride's hometown
❏ Traditional	❏ Groom's hometown
Wedding Style	**Preference**
❏ Nontraditional	❏ Other location
❏ Casual	❏ Indoor ceremony
❏ Festive	❏ Outdoor ceremony
❏ Religious	❏ Church – religious
❏ Contemporary	❏ Other – non-religious
Wedding Size	**Season**
❏ Intimate (fewer than 50)	❏ Spring
❏ Small (50 to 125)	❏ Summer
❏ Medium (125 to 250)	❏ Autumn
❏ Large (more than 250)	❏ Winter
Hour of Day	**Color Palette**
❏ Sunrise	❏ Pastels
❏ Midday	❏ Rich hues (jewel tones)
❏ Sunset	❏ All-white
❏ Evening	❏ Black and white
❏ Late night	❏ Bright hues (primary colors)
Bride's Priorities	**Groom's Priorities**
❏ Season	❏ Season
❏ Location	❏ Location
❏ Guest list	❏ Guest List
❏ Type of ceremony	❏ Type of ceremony

❏ Reception location	❏ Reception location
❏ Decorations	❏ Decorations
❏ Food and drink	❏ Food and drink
❏ Entertainment	❏ Entertainment
❏ Attire	❏ Attire
❏ Memorabilia	❏ Memorabilia
❏ Other:	❏ Other:

Again, these are just questions to get you to start building the wedding of your dreams. As you read the book, you will discover how to fill in all of the details for each aspect of the wedding ceremony and the reception. At this point, you might not know which style of wedding you want. As you go through the details of getting organized and you start researching and planning your options, your vision will morph and change until you have put together some kind of combination of the wedding that you and your fiancé have envisioned from the start.

The wedding budget, which is discussed thoroughly in Chapter 4, also tends to play a pivotal role in the style of wedding you end up having. If your budget is small, the type of wedding you plan will have to be small and inexpensive as well. This does not mean you have to sacrifice your dreams based solely on your wedding budget because throughout this book you will find tips, tricks, and advice on how to get the second wedding of your dreams without emptying your bank account at the same time.

You also can find a copy of the preliminary worksheet in the Appendix. Rip it out of the book, write on it in the book, or make a photocopy of it to use as a jumping off point for planning your wedding.

CASE STUDY: PUTTING THE PERSONAL TOUCH TO YOUR WEDDING CEREMONY

Heartfelt Ministries
Kelly K. Hunt
3411 Hoffman Dr. #2 Plover, WI 54467
715-343-2808
revkelly@heartfeltministries.net
www.heartfeltministries.net

Heartfelt Ministries has been providing wedding officiant services to Central Wisconsin since 2007. About half of all the weddings Heartfelt Ministries do are second (or third, etc.) weddings — approximately 200 second weddings per year. The typical bride and groom that come to Heartfelt Ministries for their wedding services are both second timers, but for the remaining couples, there is a 50/50 split on the number of grooms versus the number of brides walking down the aisle again.

Sometimes the bride and groom come from different religious backgrounds, but, typically, they are both Christian. When religious differences occur, Heartfelt Ministries takes traditions from both religions and incorporates them in the same ceremony. For example, if the couple is Christian and Jewish, a reading comes from the Old Testament to incorporate both religions, the lighting of a unity candle is a Christian element, and the breaking of the glass refers to the Jewish religion.

Another difference of a second wedding is during the introduction and foundation of marriage. Heartfelt Ministries talks about new beginnings and how the couple needs to celebrate their past, as well as their future, because it is what brought them to get married. In a first marriage, Heartfelt Ministries' ceremonies talk more about how marriage is a commitment, but someone entering into a second marriage already knows that and would rather talk about a new start.

Second weddings tend to be simpler and more about the ceremony and the words used to bind them together in marriage rather than the cake, dress, or dinner like some first weddings tend to be. Also, Kelly K. Hunt, in her role as an officiant, feels more like a coach rather than a director. In other words, second wedding couples have already been there and want to do something that is about their love, not about what people tell them it should be.

CHAPTER FOUR

Get Organized — Plan for the Planning

Some people are naturally organized individuals, and others seem to be organizationally challenged. When it comes to planning a wedding, however, organizational skills come in handy. If you have been through the process of planning a first wedding, you already know what a complex and detailed process it can be. The key to planning a successful second wedding is to get organized and stay organized throughout the entire planning process — from beginning to end. In this chapter, you are going to learn how to put together an organizational system that works for you.

In addition, this chapter will teach you how to put together a wedding budget and what expenses to consider when assembling it. Not only do you need to learn how to put the budget together, but you also need to know how to manage it and work with it. The rest of the chapter delves into how to choose the wedding date and how to consider venues that meet the style of the wedding you are planning.

Finally, you will learn about putting together the wedding guest list, including adding any members of your ex's family who should be invited to the wedding. Some couples choose to invite their ex-spouses and even former in-laws. This depends on the relationship the two of you have with your exes and might be a move you choose to take to benefit your children.

Setting Up an Organizational Planning System

Each bride organizes her planning system in a way that works best for her. This section will cover some of the options to consider and those that have worked for the brides who have come before you. Weigh the pros and cons of each system, and then choose the one that seems to fit your way of doing things.

Your filing system

The best filing systems are often the easiest. Label your file folders, and use them to organize all your wedding information. You will be happy you set this up as you begin to acquire increased amounts of wedding paraphernalia. You should have a file folder for each portion of the planning process, including:

- **Ceremony location** — Store information here about locations you are considering. After you choose your ceremony location, keep a file on rules, fees, contacts, and any other pertinent information related to the location.

- **Ceremony music** — When you and your fiancé have chosen the music for your ceremony, keep a note of it in this file. You are likely to receive music suggestions from family and friends that can be filed here for later reference.

- **Reception location** — It can take several visits to many different establishments before deciding on the location for your reception. Each location you visit will have pamphlets, price sheets, and other documentation for your file.

- **Reception music** — When you and your fiancé have chosen music for your reception, keep a note of it in this file. As you interview bands, singers, and disc jockeys, save their information and any specific songs or CDs you want to remember.

- **Caterer/food** — Keep track of menus, pricing lists, and services offered.

- **Wedding cake** — Pictures of cakes you like, bakeries you are interested in, and flavor preferences for you and your fiancé should go in this file. When you choose your bakery and wedding cake, all information also should be filed.

- **Stationery** — Invitations, thank-you cards, and program notes should be filed. Catalogs easily can be slipped into the file, as well as samples of paper you particularly like and ideas for designs, verses, and companies you are interested in.

- **Flowers** — Make note of your favorite blooms, ideas for your bouquet, decorations, and other florist arrangements in this file. As you see pictures of arrangements that appeal to you, cut them out and save them for reference here. Also, as you visit florists, local and Internet suppliers, list the shop names, the person who assisted you, and your impressions.

- **Photographer** — Good photographers book up far in advance. As you receive recommendations, brochures, advertisements, and other literature on photographers, you will want to file it for reference.

- **Wedding dress** — This is the fun one. As you flip through bridal magazines and see dresses you fall in love with, clip the pictures out, and save them. When you purchase your gown, the paperwork should go here, along with a photo of the dress itself — it will help your florist immensely in creating and designing your bouquet. Fitting information also can go here.

- **Bridesmaids' dresses** — Save a picture of the dress your bridesmaids are wearing along with a record of each of their sizes. Swatches of the fabric are also a good idea, again for the florist to use when creating and designing their bouquets. Fitting information can be added.

- **Groom and groomsmen's attire** — Clip out photos of **tuxedos** you and your fiancé are partial to for this file. Rental establishments and fitting information also should be saved.

- **Transportation** — If you plan to hire or rent a specific vehicle for transportation to and from the wedding, the reception, and possibly the airport, keep all related information in this file.

- **Memorabilia** — As you search for wedding mementos for yourself and for your guests, clip out pictures, notes of things you especially like, and various vendors.

- **Miscellaneous** — If anything in this file begins to take on too great of a proportion, create a new file for it.

The notebook

Some brides create their own wedding planners using notebooks. Once the notebook is assembled, it becomes your wedding bible, and you should have it with you at all times and take it with you wherever you go. After all, you never know when you will run across something that pertains to your wedding.

To set up a wedding notebook, you need:

- A 2-inch, three-ring binder (optional: has clear pockets on the front and back of binder)
- Notebook dividers (two packages)
- Pencil case made for a three-ring binder
- Package of plastic covers made for three-ring binders
- Pens and pencils
- Notebook paper with holes, or plain paper punched with a three-hole punch

Choose a notebook style and color that you like and feel comfortable carrying with you during the entire planning process. If you choose a notebook that has the clear plastic pockets on the front and back of the binder, you can create and print a page on your computer to be a cover for the notebook. For example, it might have wedding rings on it and say "Kylie and Jason's Wedding." If you already have the wedding date, you might want to add this to your cover design as well.

Next, place a divider in the notebook for each section of the wedding. You will need to label a tab and divider for:

- Budget
- Guest list
- Venue
- Invitations and stationery
- Flowers
- Entertainment
- Food and beverage/catering
- Favors
- Attire
- Honeymoon
- Miscellaneous

In each section, add a clear plastic cover into the notebook. The clear plastic cover allows you to slide small items, samples, and pictures into the section they belong. For example, when you have chosen the dresses your bridesmaids will be wearing, you can slide a sample of the gown fabric in the attire clear plastic cover. Then, when you are meeting with the venue or the linen provider and you are trying to choose linen napkins that match the color of the dresses, you can slide out the material sample and use it to match the linens.

When you go through magazines and see a picture of something you like, rip it out, and add it to the appropriate section of your notebook. If you are walking through a store or a guest at another wedding and you see something you like, take a picture of it with your camera or camera phone, and slide it into your notebook for future reference.

Place some notebook paper in each section, so you can write notes. Place the full notebook pencil case at the beginning of the notebook so that you always will have a writing instrument available. When you get to the point when you have contracts with vendors, the floor plan of the venue, and your guest list, all of this also will be added to the notebook in the appropriate section. For right now, you simply are getting organized so you are ready and able to attack the planning process.

The planner

Another option is to head out to your favorite bookstore. Go to the wedding section and find the selection of wedding planners available. You will notice that these planners are separated into sections just like the wedding notebook with a three-ring binder. The majority of these store bought planners have dividers, pockets, checklists, and guides. These guides can cost $30 to $100, depending on which planner you choose to buy. With the advice in this book, creating the notebook might cost you only $20 to $25 to create.

> **Cost-saving tip:** Creating a wedding notebook is a less expensive way to create and use a wedding planner you can buy at the store. Because you have this book to guide you through the planning process, you do not need a planner; you can create your own planner and save money in the process.

Software programs

Wedding planner software programs are also available to help you plan the second wedding of your dreams. The advantage of a software program is the organizational system is already set up for you. You can go through and input the information into the software program, and it will keep track of everything for you. The disadvantages of software programs are that they are not portable, and these programs can be expensive — in the hundreds of dollars.

You might even find that using some combination of these methods works for you. For example, you might photocopy the checklists out of this book for various sections and place them into your notebook. You might opt to pay for an online service that allows your wedding guests to RSVP online. You can print this list out and keep a hard copy in your notebook to combine it with RSVPs that come in the old-fashioned way.

Setting the Budget

Now, it is time to talk about the integral part of planning any second wedding, and that is the budget. The first step in setting the budget is to bring together all of the resources contributing to the wedding. These will be gift contributions from friends and family, the two partners' salaries, and any savings they want to put toward the big day. These resources could depend on whether one of you has been married before, which of you has been married before, or whether both of you have been married before. For example, if it is the groom's first wedding, the groom's parents might be willing to shirk tradition and pay for the wedding of the couple instead of having the bride's family do it again. In many cases, the couple even pays for their own wedding, so it removes the tradition altogether.

Write down all of the sources of income for the wedding budget. Also, indicate the amount coming from each source. This allows you to obtain a big picture view of the total amount of money you have to work with when planning your wedding. It certainly does not mean you have to spend all of the money you set aside for your wedding. It is simply a guideline you should use to avoid overspending or going over your budget.

One of the easiest ways to create and manage your wedding budget is to use a computer spreadsheet because it allows you to create the budget so it works for you, and it allows you to make changes and fill in information as you obtain it. For example, you can create a row for each expense in the wedding. Then, you can create a column for money you have budgeted for the item and another column for the amount you actually spend. Finally, you can create a column on the difference in the amount you budgeted versus how much you spend. This allows you to reallocate funds from one area of the budget to another, if necessary. You also can print out the spreadsheet and add it to your notebook, so you have the latest version with you wherever you go.

There are two ways for approaching setting the budget for your wedding.

1. You can total up all of the money source amounts you have and then work backwards to assign an estimated expense for each item on your list.

2. You can assign a cost to each item on your wedding list and then total it to find out how much money you need to pay for the wedding you want to throw.

See Appendix B for a sample budget spreadsheet setup. For now, here is a sample budget worksheet to help you set up your expected wedding expenses, how much you spend when you purchase the item or service, and the difference between the two.

Budget Worksheet

Item Estimated Cost vs. Actual Cost			
	Estimated Cost	Actual Cost	Difference
Wedding planner	$	$	$
Wedding gown	$	$	$
Wedding lingerie	$	$	$
Hair accessories	$	$	$
Wedding shoes	$	$	$
Accessories	$	$	$
Hair	$	$	$
Hairdresser gratuity	$	$	$
Makeup	$	$	$
Makeup gratuity	$	$	$
Groom's attire	$	$	$
Groom's shoes	$	$	$
Ceremony site fee	$	$	$
Officiant fee	$	$	$
Officiant gratuity	$	$	$
Ceremony programs	$	$	$
Religious items	$	$	$
Ceremony decorations	$	$	$
Ceremony musicians	$	$	$
Chair rental	$	$	$
Vehicle rental	$	$	$
Driver gratuity	$	$	$
Other ceremony expenses	$	$	$
Groom's wedding ring	$	$	$

Item Estimated Cost vs. Actual Cost			
	Estimated Cost	Actual Cost	Difference
Bride's wedding ring	$	$	$
Reception site fee	$	$	$
Catering	$	$	$
Caterer's gratuity	$	$	$
Server's gratuity	$	$	$
Liquor costs	$	$	$
Bartender gratuity	$	$	$
Wedding cake	$	$	$
Cake topper	$	$	$
Groom's cake	$	$	$
Reception decorations	$	$	$
Reception musicians	$	$	$
Musician gratuity	$	$	$
Chair/table rental	$	$	$
Dance floor rental	$	$	$
Guest book	$	$	$
Toasting glasses	$	$	$
Cake knife/server	$	$	$
Tent rental	$	$	$
Valet parking	$	$	$
Valet gratuity	$	$	$
Coat check gratuity	$	$	$
Bridal bouquet	$	$	$
Bridal party bouquets	$	$	$
Flower girl flowers	$	$	$

Item Estimated Cost vs. Actual Cost			
	Estimated Cost	Actual Cost	Difference
Ring bearer pillow	$	$	$
Mother/grandmother corsages	$	$	$
Bridal party boutonnieres	$	$	$
Father/grandfather boutonnieres	$	$	$
Other flowers	$	$	$
Photographer	$	$	$
Videographer	$	$	$
Save-the-date cards	$	$	$
Wedding invitations	$	$	$
Postage	$	$	$
Calligrapher	$	$	$
Thank-you cards	$	$	$
Personalized napkins/matchbooks	$	$	$
Wedding favors	$	$	$
Wedding insurance	$	$	$
Bridesmaids luncheon	$	$	$
Bridal party gifts	$	$	$
Parents' gifts	$	$	$
Rehearsal expenses	$	$	$
Rehearsal dinner	$	$	$
Honeymoon	$	$	$
Honeymoon insurance	$	$	$
Other expenses	$	$	$
Grand Total	$	$	$

Choosing the Date

Couples choose the wedding date in many different ways. Some couples choose a date because it is a meaningful date for them, such as the day they met, the day they got engaged, their first kiss, or some other important day. If you have a venue chosen, or a couple of possible venue choices, you might choose a date based solely on availability.

There are two tips to heed when choosing a wedding date. First, choose your first, second, and third date options. This way when you start shopping for venues and you find one that you like, if the venue is already booked for your first choice date, you have at least two other dates from which to choose.

Second, if budget is a concern, try to pick days of the week or seasons of the year that are less expensive. For example, Friday and Sunday weddings are less expensive than Saturday night weddings. Wedding ceremonies and receptions that take place during the week, such as a destination wedding off on a tropical island, might be less expensive than a weekend wedding. June is one of the most popular wedding months, which also means wedding vendors tend to charge a premium. Choosing a wedding in a less popular month, such as November or January, also can save you money.

One other thing to keep in mind when choosing a wedding date is the cost associated with the date. For example, certain seasons and times of year are more expensive when booking a wedding than other times of the year. For example, in August in Florida, weddings are much less expensive because the weather is so hot that many people opt not to get married in the dog days of summer. The same holds true in the middle of winter in Michigan. Springs days in Florida might be booked everywhere, while the same holds true for spring days in Michigan.

Choosing the Time

The time of your wedding is essential to your wedding budget and to the style of your ceremony. Consider the following tips when deciding your wedding time:

- Wedding services and sites charge rates depending on the time of day of your wedding. Because of this, you might find it less expensive to be married in the morning rather than the afternoon or evening. As you consider different locales, do not forget to ask if there is a time factor in relation to their fees. If, for example, you are having a late-night wedding, you might be charged extra for cleanup if the staff has to arrive the following morning to begin. This could equal a full extra day rental fee. Pay close attention, and ask whenever you are unsure about any potential charges.

- The time of your wedding and reception reflects the formality of your wedding. Tradition dictates that a morning ceremony, with possibly a brunch reception, will cost far less than an elegantly formal candlelit ceremony with a catered five-course sit-down dinner reception. You and your fiancé should discuss what type of reception you both want and use that as a guide to choosing your ceremony time.

- An early afternoon wedding also can save you money. Instead of having a full dinner reception, you could have an afternoon tea or a selection of hors d'oeuvres. Both of these suggestions can be presented in an extremely elegant manner. Food tops the list for cost, so if your budget is especially tight, this is one way to shave a considerable amount off your bottom line.

- In addition to food, alcohol is a budget-breaker for many couples planning their wedding. A late-morning or early afternoon wedding will allow you to serve only nonalcoholic beverages.

- If your heart is set on having your wedding outside, a late morning or early evening wedding will offer milder temperatures in the summer. You can see a listing of typical weather, based on location, here: **www.weather.com/activities/events/weddings/setthedate/ index.html?from=wed_welcome**.

- Depending on the locality of your wedding and reception, certain times of day might mean heavier traffic affecting the arrival times for your guests, the officiant, and your cake, as well as you and your fiancé.

- Consider your guests' schedules when setting the time for your wedding. If you decide on a Friday evening ceremony, you might want to push the start time to 7 p.m., rather than 6, so people coming from work have time to go home before arriving at the ceremony location.

- Another benefit to having an earlier ceremony and reception is greater flexibility for you and your fiancé. You will be able to leave for your honeymoon the same day as your wedding, rather than waiting until the following morning.

- You can choose the date and then locate sites and services that are available. This is the more traditional option.

- You can narrow down a season and a month and then set your wedding date based on the availability of the ceremony and reception site.

Creating a Guest List

Creating a guest list for a second wedding can get a little complicated because one or both of you might want to invite people from your previous marriage, even your ex-spouse. Before getting into the complexities of putting together a guest list, it is best to start with the basics. Again, creating a guest list in a spreadsheet is a great way to add, delete, make changes easily, and even keep track of RSVPs as they come. If you have meal choices, you can even include this as one of the columns of the spreadsheet to make your life easier when meeting with the caterer or the venue responsible for preparing the food.

Especially when it comes to a second wedding, only include guests you want and need to invite. This is typically close family members and friends. It is not necessary or expected to invite second and third cousins, or members of your extended family, especially if you never talk to them or do not have a close relationship with them. The smaller the guest list, the more money you end up saving.

The best way to assemble the guest list is to make your own and have your fiancé create his own guest list. Especially if you use a spreadsheet program, you can eliminate duplicate guests quickly and easily. Then, you can have each of your parents assemble the list of guests they would like to invite. Parents paying for the second wedding have more say in invited guests. Even if you are paying for the wedding, having your parents assemble guest lists as well helps ensure you have not forgotten to include anyone.

> **Organization tip:** Include you, your fiancé, and your bridal party on the guest list. Your bridal party should receive wedding invitations, and for food and beverage purposes, including everyone, even members of the wedding, provides accurate figures.

Inviting your ex: When it is and is not OK

One of the great debates for a second wedding is if you should invite your ex-spouse to the wedding. It is primarily a preference and a discussion you and your fiancé should have before making a final decision. Primarily, there are two times when it is a good idea to invite your ex to the wedding:

1. When you have a good relationship with him or her and you have children together

2. To illustrate to your children that their parents are still on good terms

If you and you ex-spouse do not get along and cannot even be in the same room together without an argument breaking out, it is best to keep the ex off the list. If you do not have any children with your ex, there really is not a need to add him or her to the guest list, whether you get along or not.

Inviting members of your ex's family

Similar rules apply when it comes to inviting members of your ex-spouse's family. If you have children with your ex and you have maintained a good relationship with your ex in-laws, it is acceptable to invite them to the wedding. If you have children with your ex but do not get along with his or her parents, it might be best to omit them from the guest list. If you do not have children with your ex-spouse, there really is not a reason why his or her parents need to be there.

Inviting friends from your first marriage

Any friends you had before marrying your ex can make the wedding guest list. If it is a friend you acquired during your first marriage, for example if you became friends with the wife of your ex-husband's friend, then this is a situational decision. You might choose to invite them because you want them there, but if they feel this might cause a rift with your ex-spouse, then they might politely decline. If you no longer speak to the friends, however, it is wise to keep them off the guest list, for monetary and emotional reasons.

Considering the Venues

Generally, you choose a venue, or location, for the wedding ceremony and another for the wedding reception. Start by making a list of venues that match the style of wedding you and your fiancé have chosen. For example, if you have chosen a destination wedding, consider destinations such as tropical resorts, mountain resorts, or other destinations that fit in with the wedding style. *More examples of possible wedding venues will be covered in Chapter 7.*

> **Cost-saving tip:** You might be able to save money by having your ceremony and reception in the same location. For example, a ceremony that takes place at a synagogue with the reception to follow in the synagogue's ballroom cuts down on the cost of transportation for the bride and groom, wedding guests, and the bridal party.

As you match your venues with the style of wedding, the wedding dates you have chosen also come into play. Just as you have one primary wedding date and a couple of backup dates, you should use the same system with your venues. Your first choice venue might be booked solid for the next year, which means even if you have a few backup dates, unless you want to wait two years to get married, you might have to move on to your next venue choice.

Getting organized up front and staying organized throughout the wedding planning process will save you a lot of stress, hair pulling, and even nervous breakdowns. Planning your wedding should be fun and exciting. When you can put your finger on the information you want and need when you need and want it, it makes planning your wedding a much more enjoyable process. After focusing on getting organized, you can then get into the details of starting to plan your wedding. Now, it is time to enlist your help — your wedding party — that is discussed in Chapter 5.

CHAPTER FIVE

The Bridal Party

Especially in a second wedding, your bridal party is more meaningful than ever to the bride and groom. First time brides and grooms often choose bridal party members that are family members  and close friends. Second time brides and grooms often put together a bridal party that might include their own children from previous relationships or opt not to have a bridal party at all. For those planning more of a traditional second wedding, this chapter discusses how to choose the bridal party. The chapter also covers how to incorporate the children from previous relationships into the wedding. You also will learn about some of the other roles that important family members or children can play in the wedding besides being in the wedding party itself.

Maid of Honor

Other than the bride and the groom, the maid (or matron) of honor is one of the most critical roles. Before the wedding, she will go with you to shop for your dress and other accessories; she can help you address invitations, organize your bridal shower, and record wedding gifts as they arrive. During the ceremony and reception, she will distribute the corsages and boutonnieres; assist you with your dress, makeup, and hair; and assist the bridesmaids with their preparation. She can hold your bouquet and your fiancé's ring, serve as an official witness to the vows, arrange your train and veil, and keep wedding attire during the honeymoon.

The Best Man

Flexibility is one trait to consider when deciding who should be the best man. Before the wedding, he will encourage your fiancé when stressed, make travel arrangements for you and your fiancé, ascertain if all fittings are completed by the groomsmen, and organize your fiancé's bachelor party. During the wedding ceremony and reception, he oversees the **ushers**, acts as an official witness to the vows, holds your ring, safeguards the marriage license, pays the honorarium to the officiant, and proposes a toast at the bridal table. After the wedding, he will return all the rented tuxedos.

Bridesmaids and Groomsmen

Bridesmaids and groomsmen make up your bridal party. Traditionally, the bride chooses her own maid of honor, matron of honor (if applicable), bridesmaids, and the flower girl. The groom, on the other hand, is traditionally responsible for picking his **best man**, groomsmen, and the ring bearer. The bride and the groom work together to make sure they have an equal number of bridesmaids and groomsmen, so walking down the aisle is balanced and correct. There also may be a discussion in which the two come to an agreement on the people each has chosen to be part of the bridal party.

Bridesmaids and groomsmen are typically people who are important to the bride and groom — they are the people the bride and groom are close to and have special connections to. The bridal party is the bride and groom's way of telling the members they are special people and that it is important to the bride and groom that these are the people acting as witnesses in sharing their special day.

The bridal party has responsibilities during both the wedding ceremony and the reception portion of the celebration. The following chart will give you a quick overview of traditional wedding party responsibilities:

The Maid of Honor	The Best Man
✓ Assists the bride with pre-wedding plans, such as scouting locations, seating plans, registering	✓ Is in charge of overseeing and making arrangements for the bachelor party
✓ Assists the bride in selecting her wedding gown and the bridesmaids' gowns	✓ Sets up time to get fitted for his personal tuxedo
✓ Purchases own gown and arranges for personal fitting of gown	✓ Ascertains if the groomsmen have been measured for their tuxes
✓ Often assists in addressing the wedding invitations	✓ Is in attendance at the wedding rehearsal and at the rehearsal dinner
✓ Plans a bridal shower for the bride	✓ Provides transportation, either by driving or hiring a driver, for the groom to the wedding ceremony
✓ Is in attendance at the wedding rehearsal and at the rehearsal dinner	✓ Brings any boxes or gifts to the ceremony and reception
✓ Ascertains if the bridesmaids are in place at their appropriate locations before the ceremony	✓ Helps the groom dress
✓ Assists the bride with makeup, hair, and dressing before the ceremony	✓ Gives the honorarium fee to the officiant
✓ Holds the bride's bouquet and the groom's wedding ring at the altar during the ceremony	✓ Holds the bride's ring during the ceremony
✓ Signs the wedding certificate	✓ Signs the wedding certificate
✓ If requested, stands in the receiving line with the bride, groom, and parents	✓ Offers the first toast to the wedding couple at the reception
✓ May offer a toast to the wedding couple at the reception	✓ Arranges transportation or drives the bride and groom to the airport or the hotel after the reception
	✓ Returns all the tuxedos to the rental facility after the reception

The Maid of Honor	The Best Man
✓ Assists the bride in any changes of clothing, such as a reception gown or a going-away outfit ✓ Helps the best man deliver gifts to the bride and groom's residence after the reception	✓ Helps the maid of honor deliver gifts to the bride and groom's residence after the reception

The Bridesmaids	The Groomsmen
✓ Help in preplanning, such as assisting in addressing the invitations ✓ Participate in the planning and carrying off of the bridal shower ✓ Purchase own gowns and arrange for personal fittings of gown ✓ Are in attendance at the wedding rehearsal and at the rehearsal dinner ✓ Circulate during the reception, talking and dancing with guests and groomsmen	✓ Help plan and attend the groom's bachelor party ✓ Arrange fittings and pay for renting personal tuxedo ✓ Escort guests to their seats at the ceremony ✓ Escort the mother of the bride and mother of the groom to their seats at the ceremony ✓ Circulate during the reception, talking and dancing with guests and the bridesmaids

Choosing the members of the bridal party is important. Think about:

- Good friends
- Family members
- Coworkers you are close to

Keep in mind when you are choosing your wedding party that you do not have to include everyone. Fortunately, there many other roles you can ask people to fill that will help them to feel important and a special part of your wedding day. Some of these roles are covered in the third section of this chapter.

Incorporating Children from Previous Marriage/Relationship

When possible, make every effort to include all of your children and the children of your spouse-to-be in the wedding. Obviously, the age of each child determines the best role they can and should play. The point of including your children in the wedding is to reassure them, especially younger ones, that you are not moving on without them, that they are still a part of your life and your new family you are forming. If you are older and your children are adults, this might be the exception to the rule. You might ask that your adult child be a part of the wedding party or fill a role in the wedding. However, adult children usually do not need the same reassurance as younger children. You still should have a conversation with your adult children to see how they feel about playing a role in the wedding to make sure you are not leaving anyone out who would like to feel included.

Babies and toddlers:

- Flower girl (up to age 8)
- Ring bearer (up to age 8)
- Include the children in your vows by having a separate set of vows to the children, in addition to the vows for the husband and wife (bride says vows to husband's children and vice versa)
- Dressed similar to the bride or bridesmaid, but cared for by a parent or close friend during the ceremony; sit in the front row, so the child is close to his or her parent

Ages 9 to 15

- Bride can have her children give her away
- Junior bridesmaid
- Junior groomsmen
- Usher
- Hand out wedding programs to guests at ceremony
- Remind guests to sign the **guest book**
- Hand out directions to the reception
- Have the children participate in the lighting of the **unity candle**
- Include the children in your vows
- Pass around petals or birdseed to throw at the bride and groom as they leave church/reception
- Direct guests to the gift table

Ages 16+

- Bride can have her children give her away
- Bridesmaid
- Groomsmen
- Maid of honor
- Best man
- Have the children participate in the lighting of the unity candle
- Include the children in your vows
- Reader
- Load wedding gifts into the car to deliver to the house

Although this is not a comprehensive list, it gives you some idea of how you can include your children. You can get as creative as you want. If your teenage son has a band, maybe you can have them perform at the wedding. If your daughter has a beautiful voice, she can sing one of the songs. If one or more of your children is crafty, they can help you assemble the wedding favors, put together the place card holders, or even assemble the flower centerpieces, if you are going the do-it-yourself route on one or more areas of your wedding.

The flower girl

If there are one, two, or more special little girls in your life, you may decide to have flower girls. Their only responsibility is during the ceremony when they walk down the aisle sprinkling flower petals on the ground to signify your entrance. If you would like to give them additional duties, things such as helping with the gift table, the guest registry, and handing out favors are all possibilities.

The ring bearer

If you or your fiancé have a young boy, you may decide to include him as the ring bearer. He carries a pillow with the wedding rings of the bride and groom sewn on it. Many couples decide to have the flower girl and the ring bearer walk side by side.

Mother of the Bride

Your mother's main function in your wedding is to help you plan according to your tastes and style. If you prefer to hand the reigns over to mom, you certainly can, but most brides prefer to guide their wedding their way. You and your mother might want to take some time to go over the following list of responsibilities and personalize it for your wedding and your wishes.

Before the wedding, the mother of the bride:

1. Traditionally hosts the first engagement party.
2. Customarily contributes financially to the wedding budget.
3. Assists you and your fiancé in choosing the venue for your wedding ceremony and for the reception.
4. Assists you in developing your family's guest list for the ceremony.
5. Discusses various possibilities for different types of ceremonies with you, including family or traditional customs.
6. May help you shop for and choose your wedding gown and other accessories.

7. Chooses her dress for the ceremony. She may coordinate formality and color with the mother of the groom.

8. Plans and hosts a bridal shower along with the maid of honor or a secondary shower.

9. Assists you in your preparations before the ceremony, including your dress, cosmetics, hair, and anything else you may need.

10. Can help babysit the children if you have wedding errands to run.

During the ceremony, the mother of the bride:

1. May assist in last-minute ceremony troubleshooting.

2. Is escorted down the aisle to her seat by an usher, son, or your father immediately before the ceremony begins for a Christian ceremony. If the ceremony is Jewish, she will walk down the aisle with you and your father to stand beneath the chuppah.

3. Will be escorted back down the aisle after the ceremony if you are having a Christian ceremony. If your ceremony is Jewish, she will walk in the recessional with your father.

4. Stands in the receiving line with you and your husband after the ceremony.

5. Can take charge of younger children during the wedding to make sure they behave and are dressed and ready on time.

After the ceremony, the mother of the bride:

1. May assist in coordinating vendors at the reception.

2. Sits in an honored place at the parents' table.

3. May host a post-wedding brunch or afternoon tea.

The Bride's Father

Your father's function in your wedding will depend largely on how much he wants to be involved and how much you want him involved. There are no hard and fast rules for the father of the bride assisting in the planning of the wedding, but there is also nothing to say he should not. Traditionally, the father of the bride has the following responsibilities:

Before the wedding, the father of the bride:

1. Hosts an engagement party to celebrate the upcoming nuptials. The bride's family traditionally hosts the first engagement party.

2. Customarily contributes financially to the wedding budget

3. May assist you and your fiancé in choosing the venue for your wedding ceremony and for the reception.

4. Rents his own tuxedo and may assist with the rental coordination of the best man and the groomsmen.

5. Assists in picking up out-of-town guests as they arrive from the airport and shuttling them to their hotel. He also may help arrange transportation to and from the wedding and reception.

6. Can help babysit the children if you have wedding errands to run.

During the ceremony, the father of the bride:

1. May escort your mother to her seat immediately before the ceremony for Christian ceremonies, though it is appropriate for a son or usher to do this instead. For Jewish ceremonies, your father will walk with you and your mother down the aisle to stand beneath the chuppah.

2. May "give you away" to your fiancé during the ceremony.

3. Will escort your mother down the aisle after the ceremony if you are having a Christian ceremony. If your ceremony is Jewish, he will walk in the recessional with your mother.

4. Stands in the receiving line with you and your husband after the ceremony.

5. Can take charge of younger children during the wedding to make sure they behave and are dressed and ready on time.

After the ceremony, the father of the bride:

1. May choose to give a welcome speech.

2. Sits in an honored place at the parents' table.

3. Toasts you and your husband after the best man's speech.

4. Will dance the traditional father and daughter dance at the reception.

5. May pay remaining vendor fees at the end of the reception.

6. May host a post-wedding brunch or afternoon tea with your mother.

The Groom's Mother

Take some time to talk with your future mother-in-law and customize a personal approach to her role in your wedding.

Before the wedding, the mother of the groom:

1. May choose to contact your mother, if they have not previously met, to set up a luncheon or another first meeting. If they are acquainted, she still may choose to set up a luncheon to celebrate.

2. Should attend an engagement party.

3. May decide to host a secondary engagement party after your family's party is complete.

4. May contribute to the wedding budget.

5. Will assist your fiancé with a guest list from their side of the family.

6. May discuss possibilities of different types of ceremonies with you, including family or traditional customs.

7. May help you shop for and choose your wedding gown if you feel comfortable with her.

8. Chooses her dress for the ceremony. She may coordinate formality and color with the mother of the bride.

9. Will plan and host the rehearsal dinner.

10. Can help babysit the children if you have wedding errands to run.

During the ceremony, the mother of the groom:

1. Is escorted down the aisle by an usher, son, or your fiancé's father to her seat immediately before the ceremony begins for a Christian ceremony. If the ceremony is Jewish, she will walk down the aisle with your fiancé and his father to stand beneath the chuppah.

2. Will be escorted back down the aisle after the ceremony if you are having a Christian ceremony. If your ceremony is Jewish, she will walk in the recessional with your fiancé's father.

3. Stands in the receiving line with you and your husband after the ceremony.

4. Can take charge of younger children during the wedding to make sure they behave and are dressed and ready on time.

After the ceremony, the mother of the groom:

1. Sits in an honored place at the parents' table.

2. Dances with your fiancé during the mother and son dance.

3. Attends the post-wedding brunch your mother and father host and hosts one herself with your fiancé's father.

The Groom's Father

You and your fiancé can bring your future father-in-law into the planning of the wedding if you so choose and if he would like to help. The traditional role of the groom's father is as follows.

Before the wedding, the father of the groom:

1. Should attend the engagement party.

2. May assist your fiancé's mother in hosting a secondary engagement party after your family's hosted party.

3. May contribute to the wedding budget.

4. Will rent his own tuxedo.

5. Will help plan and host the rehearsal dinner.

6. May travel with your fiancé and the best man to the ceremony.

7. Can help babysit the children if you have wedding errands to run.

During the ceremony, the father of the groom:

1. May escort your fiancé's mother down the aisle to her seat immediately before the ceremony begins if it is a Christian ceremony. Alternately, an usher or another son may perform this duty. If the ceremony is Jewish, he will walk down the aisle with your fiancé and his mother to stand beneath the chuppah.

2. Will escort your fiancé's mother back down the aisle after the ceremony if you are having a Christian ceremony. If your ceremony is Jewish, he will walk in the recessional with your fiancé's mother.

3. Stands in the receiving line with you and your husband after the ceremony.

4. Can take charge of younger children during the wedding to make sure they behave and are dressed and ready on time.

After the ceremony, the father of the groom

1. Sits in an honored place at the parents' table.

2. May make a welcoming speech.

3. May toast you and your fiancé.

4. May pay off remaining balances with wedding vendors.

5. Hosts the post-wedding brunch.

If you prefer minimal assistance from your parents, be sure to communicate your wishes clearly from the beginning.

Including Important People in Other Aspects

Just as you can find alternative roles for your children, special people in your life can fill roles in your wedding in numerous ways beyond being in the bridal party. Several of the options that apply to your kids also can apply to other people you want to include in your wedding celebration.

You need a lot of help leading up to and during the planning process of the wedding. This is another great way to ask a good friend to help you with your big day. Ask one of your favorite coworkers to go dress shopping with you instead of or in addition to having your maid of honor or bridesmaids. Think about the talents of the people in your life and think about how you can apply those to your wedding.

For example, if a cousin you are close to is a graphic designer, ask him or her to help design your wedding invitations and any stationery you plan to use. When you are planning a wedding, there is always something to be done or an errand to run. Enlist a good friend or family member to help you manage some of this, such as picking up wedding favors from the store, assembling the favors, or even dropping off the rented tuxedos after the wedding is over.

Your good friends and family members will understand, especially for as second wedding, that you cannot find a place for everyone in the wedding ceremony. This does not mean, however, you cannot ask for their help and make them feel as if they are a big part of your special day. Ask them to babysit your kids while you are running errands for the wedding or have the kids stay with them while you head off on your honeymoon. You can even hand them your guest list and ask them to track down missing mailing addresses to help you get ready to address and mail out the invitations. Assembling and stamping invitations are other special roles people can play in your wedding. In essence, the possibilities are endless.

In general, second weddings have smaller bridal parties than first weddings. In the end, however, it is a preference of the bride and groom. If one or both of you have children, it is imperative that you find an age-appropriate role for each child to help them feel as if they are part of the wedding. In the end, you need all the help you can get when planning your wedding. Even if you cannot include everyone in the ceremony, find other ways to use the talents of your friends and family members who want to help.

In order to cement your bridal party roles and make sure you have all the information you need for the people who will be assisting you on your big day, fill out or have your party fill out this contact sheet to help you keep in contact.

Bridal Party Contact Sheet

Females

Role: ❑ Maid of honor ❑ Bridesmaid ❑ Flower girl

Name: _____

Address: _____

Telephone: _____ Cell phone: _____

Email address: _____

Role: ❑ Maid of honor ❑ Bridesmaid ❑ Flower girl

Name: _____

Address: _____

Telephone: _____ Cell phone: _____

Email address: _____

Role: ❑ Maid of honor ❑ Bridesmaid ❑ Flower girl

Name: _____

Address: _____

Telephone: _____ Cell phone: _____

Email address: _____

Role: ❑ Maid of honor ❑ Bridesmaid ❑ Flower girl

Name: _____

Address: _____

Telephone: _____ Cell phone: _____

Email address: _____

Role: ❑ Maid of honor ❑ Bridesmaid ❑ Flower girl

Name: _____

Address: _____

Telephone: _____ Cell phone: _____

Email address: _____

Role: ❑ Maid of honor ❑ Bridesmaid ❑ Flower girl

Name: _____

Address: _____

Telephone: _____ Cell phone: _____

Email address: _____

Role: ❑ Maid of honor ❑ Bridesmaid ❑ Flower girl

Name: _____

Address: _____

Telephone: _____ Cell phone: _____

Email address: _____

Role: ❑ Maid of honor ❑ Bridesmaid ❑ Flower girl

Name: _____

Address: _____

Telephone: _____ Cell phone: _____

Email address: _____

Males

Role: ❑ Best man ❑ Groomsman ❑ Usher ❑ Ring bearer

Name: _____

Address: _____

Telephone: _____ Cell phone: _____

Email address: _____

Role: ❑ Best man ❑ Groomsman ❑ Usher ❑ Ring bearer

Name: _____

Address: _____

Telephone: _____ Cell phone: _____

Email address: _____

Role: ❑ Best man ❑ Groomsman ❑ Usher ❑ Ring bearer

Name: _____

Address: _____

Telephone: _____ Cell phone: _____

Email address: _____

Role: ❑ Best man ❑ Groomsman ❑ Usher ❑ Ring bearer

Name: _____

Address: _____

Telephone: _____ Cell phone: _____

Email address: _____

Bride's Parents

Mother of the bride

Name: _____

Address: _____

Telephone: _____ Cell phone: _____

Email address: _____

Father of the bride

Name: _____

Address: _____

Telephone: _____ Cell phone: _____

Email address: _____

Groom's Parents

Mother of the groom

Name: _____

Address: _____

Telephone: _____ Cell phone: _____

Email address: _____

Father of the groom

Name: _____

Address: _____

Telephone: _____ Cell phone: _____

Email address: _____

Once you complete your bridal party contact information sheet, place it in your wedding notebook, planner, or other planning system for easy access.

Witnesses

If you decide not to have a bridal party, you still need two witnesses to sign your marriage certificate. Witnesses can be anyone 18 years old or older. For example, one couple that had a small beach wedding  in Florida simply asked some tourists walking on the beach if they would act as their witnesses. Witnesses do have to stand and watch the wedding ceremony and exchange of vows. The witnesses are signing their name to the certificate to verify that both parties willingly entered into the marriage contract.

Generally, most brides and grooms do not choose strangers. You can ask close friends, family members, or even coworkers to act as witnesses to your wedding. If you are having a small wedding, you still might wish to choose two witnesses you have a special relationship with, although, frankly, any adult witness will do.

Money-Saving Tips

Money-saving tip #1: Smaller wedding parties equal savings. If you have a large wedding party, you will have that many more gifts to purchase. If you are paying for accommodations for out-of-town attendants, the more you have, the more you pay. Each attendant can equal upward of $200 out of your budget.

Money-saving tip #2: Consider having only a maid of honor and a best man without any bridesmaids or groomsmen to save on costs. Male relatives or friends can act as ushers.

Money-saving tip #3: If you know several young girls, consider having only flower girls. Your wedding would be unique, and the wedding processional would be adorable.

Money-saving tip #4: When choosing your attendants, especially your maid of honor and best man, pick responsible individuals who truly will help. You will save time, which is worth money, if you have people on your side that will be happy to help. If your attendants are irresponsible, you likely will waste a good deal of your precious time making sure things are getting accomplished.

Money-saving tip #5: Choose attendants who communicate well with you. An essential component of saving money is organization. You will need to be able to communicate schedule updates and changes with your wedding party, and poor communication is costly.

> **Money-saving tip #6:** Do not offer to reimburse your attendants for their attire or travel. Although this is a grand gesture and sure to be appreciated, you do not have an endless budget.
>
> **Money-saving tip #7:** Consider their budgets as well as yours. If your maid of honor has the ability to spend a large amount on her gown, but the bridesmaids you choose do not, there are sure to be recriminations.

Now that you have enlisted some help, you are well on your way to getting started. You have chosen people to witness your wedding that mean the world to you, and even ones that possess talents to help you pull off this whole planning thing. With your reinforcements in place, now it is time to learn about and prepare for the legalities of a second wedding. *All of the legal requirements you need to be aware of and what you need to do to get your marriage license are covered in Chapter 6.*

CHAPTER SIX

Legal Requirements for a Second Marriage

Unfortunately, it is time to take some of the romance out of planning your second wedding for just a moment. A marriage, while based on love, is actually a legally binding contract between a man and a woman. As of 2011, a few states even recognize marriage as a legally binding contract in same-sex marriages. Even though your excitement for the wedding is concentrated on celebrating your special day with your special someone, you also want your wedding to be recognized legally by the state or country where you are getting married. Because marriage is a legal process, there are legal documents, and you have to take legal steps to ensure your second marriage is a legal one.

In this chapter, you will discover the legal requirements of applying for the marriage license when one or both of you are divorced or a widow or widower. Some of these requirements include blood tests, divorce papers, or possibly a death certificate. The specific requirements can vary by the state and county where the ceremony will take place. The chapter covers the basics and how to find out what specific legal requirements you have to meet to get your marriage license, when to apply, how long the license is good for, and what to do with the license during and after the wedding.

Applying for the Marriage License

The first step is to apply for a marriage license. You have to have the marriage license for the wedding ceremony to take place. The first item the person performing your wedding ceremony asks for before proceeding is the marriage license. The county clerk's office at the courthouse is responsible for issuing marriage licenses. The details of obtaining the marriage license can vary from state to state and even from county to county. Contact the closest county clerk's office in the state where you intend to marry to obtain the details.

If you are having a destination wedding out of the United States, each country has its own requirements for obtaining a marriage license. Contact the U.S. embassy in the country where you are marrying to obtain the information on applying for a license. Foreign countries can take up to six months to issue marriage licenses, so make the necessary arrangements when you first start planning and well in advance of your wedding date. If you marry in a foreign country, you do not have to record your marriage license in the U.S. The marriage license is recorded in the country you marry but is recognized as a legal marriage in the U.S.

The details

One of the first things you need to find out when applying for a marriage license is if the marriage license is good for any county in the state. For example, if you intend to get married in Key West, in Monroe County. If you live and apply for your marriage license in Miami-Dade County, the marriage license is still good for you to have a ceremony in Key West. In other words, the state of Florida allows you to apply for a marriage license at any county in the state, so you can get married anywhere in the state. Other states are not like this, so you have to obtain and use the marriage license for the county in which you choose to marry.

The second question to ask the county clerk's office is about the waiting period. Some states do not have a waiting period, which means as soon as you obtain a marriage license, you can go get married. Other states have waiting periods that range from days to weeks. Apply for and obtain your marriage license early, so you will have it on the day of the wedding.

The third detail you should find out is how long the marriage license is good for. Most marriage licenses are valid for 30 days. This means that you have 30 days from the time you obtain the marriage license for the wedding to take place. If the wedding does not take place before the expiration date, then you have to apply for a new marriage license, which means going through the entire process all over again.

Supporting documentation required

Again, find out what documentation you need to bring with you to apply for the marriage license. Typically, the bride and groom each must have a government-issued photo I.D. If one or both of you has been married before but is divorced, you also will need to bring a copy of your divorce decree. If one or both of you is a widow/widower, you will need to bring a copy of your deceased spouse's death certificate. Check ahead of time to see what form of payment the marriage license department accepts. Some only accept cash, while others accept credit cards, checks, or cash. You also may need to bring a copy of your birth certificate. When you get to the clerk's office, you need to complete the marriage license application, supply the documentation, and pay the fee. If there is a waiting period, you will have to come back to pick up the marriage license later.

Blood tests

The majority of the states no longer require blood tests to apply for a marriage license. A couple of states, however, still require them. If your state requires blood testing, you each need to bring the results of your blood tests in addition to the other documentation that your state requires.

According to U.S. Marriage Laws (**www.usmarriagelaws.com**), the following chart illustrates which states require blood tests, along with the waiting period for obtaining your marriage license.

State Directory	Waiting Period	Blood Tests
Alabama	None	No
Alaska	3 days from time of application	No
Arizona	None	No
Arkansas	None	No
California	None	No
Colorado	None	No
Connecticut	None	Yes
Delaware	1 day for residents; 4 days for nonresidents	No
District of Columbia	5 days	No

State Directory	Waiting Period	Blood Tests
Florida	None	No
Georgia	None	No
Hawaii	None	No
Idaho	None	No
Illinois	1 day	No
Indiana	None	Yes
Iowa	3 days from time of application	No
Kansas	3 days from time of application	No
Kentucky	None	No
Louisiana	72 hours; out-of-state couples, none	No
Maine	3 days from time of application	No
Maryland	2 days	No
Massachusetts	3 days from time of application	No
Michigan	3 days from time of application	No
Minnesota	5 days from time of application	No
Mississippi	3 days	Yes
Missouri	None	No
Montana	None	Yes
Nebraska	None	No
Nevada	None	No
New Hampshire	3 days from time of application	No
New Jersey	72 hours	No
New Mexico	None	No
New York	24 hours from time of application	No
North Carolina	None	No

State Directory	Waiting Period	Blood Tests
North Dakota	None	No
Ohio	None	No
Oklahoma	None	No
Oregon	3 days	No
Pennsylvania	3 days from time of application	No
Rhode Island	None	No
South Carolina	1 day from application	No
South Dakota	None	No
Tennessee	None	No
Texas	72 hours	No
Utah	None	No
Vermont	None	No
Virginia	None	No
Washington	3 days from time of application	No
West Virginia	None	No
Wisconsin	6 days from time of application	No
Wyoming	None	No

Speak to the clerk of courts for the county where you are applying for your marriage license. They offer specific instructions on the steps to take and the places you can go for your blood testing. The price for the blood test depends on the clinic or blood bank you use to obtain the blood test and the results.

During and After the Wedding

Before the wedding ceremony begins, the person performing the ceremony will request the marriage license. He or she will complete the areas on the license he or she needs to complete, and then this person will hold on to the marriage license during the ceremony. Immediately following the ceremony, the bride and groom sign the marriage license. Then, the two witnesses, usually the maid of honor and best man, sign the marriage license. After the wedding, the completed marriage license must be filed with the county clerk's office. You can mail the marriage certificate in or deliver it in person. If you mail it, use a traceable method to verify its delivery. After the marriage license is recorded, the county sends you a certified copy.

The same legal requirements you have to meet for a first marriage is the same set of legal requirements you have to meet for a second marriage. The only difference is that you have to prove with legal documentation how your first marriage ended.

With the legalities of the wedding out the way, you now can inflate your romantic notions about getting married once again. Now it is time to get into the details of planning the wedding ceremony and reception. This is where the fun really begins. *Chapter 7 reveals the details you need to know to plan the ceremony portion of the wedding leading up to saying "I do."*

CHAPTER SEVEN

Saying I Do

Finally, you are getting to some of the more fun aspects of saying I do, such as saying "I Do!" Most brides kick off the wedding planning process by starting with the details of the wedding ceremony. Some of the topics the chapter covers are which types of ceremony venues to consider, who should perform the wedding ceremony, and even if you should hire a wedding planner or coordinator to help you plan the wedding. For example, the chapter discusses how to talk about and plan for religious differences between the bride and groom when choosing a venue and how to resolve these issues when choosing the ceremony location. Depending on the types of ceremony venues you are considering, this chapter also covers the types of items you might have to buy or rent, such as flower arrangements, pew decorations, chairs, an aisle runner, the tent, and more. Finally, the chapter covers the wedding vows — using traditional vows you work on with your officiant or writing your own vows.

Hire a Wedding Planner or Go it Alone?

Before you launch into the planning process, consider whether you want to hire a wedding planner to help you plan or you want to take on the planning on your own. Hiring a wedding planner has its advantages and disadvantages. The primary advantages are that they save you time and money. Wedding planners already have established relationships with reputable wedding vendors, so you can tell the planner what you are looking for, and he or she can schedule appointments with all of the vendors that fit your needs.

Even though wedding planners charge a fee for their services, they often have discounted rates with vendors. When they pass these discounts along to you, the amount of money you save is more than enough to cover the fee the planner charges. A wedding planner also can save you money by making suggestions on how to plan the wedding you want using money-saving tips and tricks. As the coordinator for the events, many wedding planners also act as the master of ceremonies to make announcements and guide guests through the wedding traditions. If your DJ or band does not have an MC, or you plan to use an iPod® for your wedding music, consider wedding planners that are willing and able to act as the MC. *More on using an iPod for your wedding music will be covered in Chapter 11.*

The primary disadvantage of hiring a wedding planner is the fee they charge. Although some do save you money in various ways that cover their fees, some do not pass along discounts to the clients but instead keep the discount from the wedding vendor as a commission for referring you. In this case, a wedding planner is an added expense. If you are interviewing wedding planners, find out how they charge and whether they will save you enough money to recoup the cost of their fees.

Success when working with a wedding planner is based on the rapport you have. You will be working with the planner over an extended period. Make sure you get along with and trust the wedding planner you choose because the two of you will become close during the planning period.

Choosing the Ceremony Venue

Choosing the ceremony venue involves considering several factors. Some of the considerations include:

- Time of the wedding
- Date of the wedding
- Season
- Theme or type of wedding
- Number of guests
- Pricing
- Whether the venue offers the items you need for the ceremony

Wedding ceremony venues or locations are limited only by your imagination. You can hold a wedding ceremony almost anywhere. Some venues have restrictions or permits, but here are some ideas to get you started.

- Church
- Synagogue

- Temple
- Park
- Museum
- Theater
- Hotel
- Bed and breakfast
- Mansion/your home/home of someone you know
- Garden
- Far-off destination
- Beach
- Yacht
- Historic sites
- Castle
- Country club
- Gazebo
- Zoo
- Cruise ship
- Winery

Some brides and grooms even choose to hold the wedding ceremony at the location where they first met. This is why you often catch news stories about couples tying the knot in the bookstore or the restaurant where they worked together.

Questions to ask for the wedding ceremony venue

Most common wedding venues have special wedding packages already prepared; so, all you will need is a brochure or an information sheet. However, some places might need a few extra questions asked. As you research and visit potential wedding ceremony venues, be sure to copy this list of questions so you get all the information you need to make this important decision:

- Is the site available on my wedding date?
- Is a standard fee charged? What is it?
- What does the site supply? (Find out what you will have to bring on your own so you can plan your rental fees.)
- Are there any restrictions involved in decorating the site?
- Are any additional fees involved in decorating the site?
- When can you decorate? How long before the ceremony?
- Are there any additional restrictions or fees in cleanup after the ceremony?
- Are there any rules regarding photography, videography, candles, flowers, or anything else that might add on additional fees?
- Is there an extra fee if I hire an outside musician, soloist, or organist?
- If the site is outdoors, do I need to purchase a special permit to have your ceremony there?
- Who is my contact person? (Ask for name, email, and phone number.) Will I be charged a fee for questions?
- Is there any discount or savings plan?

CASE STUDY: DESTINATION WEDDINGS MAKE GREAT SECOND WEDDINGS

Linnea Rufo
Bee & Thistle Inn and Spa
Lyme Street, Old Lyme, CT 06371
860-434-1667
innkeeper@beeandthistleinn.com
www.beeandthistleinn.com

CLASSIFIED CASE STUDIES
directly from the experts

Linnea Rufo from the Bee & Thistle Inn and Spa says the second wedding is more about sharing this special day with family and friends than it is the first time around. With approximately 30 percent of weddings being second marriages, Bee & Thistle Inn and Spa has had many different scenarios for a second wedding ceremony and reception. The inn has hosted second weddings that are the bride's second marriage, those who have lost their spouses and remarried, same sex marriages where at least one in the couple previously was married to someone else, and even a couple in their 80s marrying for the second time. At the Bee & Thistle Inn and Spa, couples often choose a destination style wedding in which the wedding guest list only reaches a maximum of 65 people.

When the couple is marrying for the second time, they tend to take over the Bee & Thistle Inn and Spa as their own. The couple will stay at the inn for two nights with a small group of close friends and family members. On the first night, they will have a small rehearsal dinner with a bonfire and s'mores — which creates a laid back but fun atmosphere for their wedding guests.

On the following day, the couple tends to spend the day relaxing and enjoying the surrounding area kayaking, and going to the Florence Griswold Museum. The final day at the inn includes the wedding ceremony followed by a reception, and ending with a small brunch and farewells.

Resolving religious differences

The most popular venues for wedding ceremonies are religious institutions. Each religion has its own rules and regulations on whether a second marriage can take place. For example, most Catholic churches do not allow a divorced individual to have a second wedding ceremony performed within their walls. This might lead you to think that you can have a Catholic priest perform the ceremony at another venue outside of the church. The issue is that the majority of Catholic priests do not perform wedding or any other religious ceremonies outside of the church.

Modern times, however, have seen some changes in this stance. For example, Catholic priest in Miami, Florida, performs ceremonies outside of the Catholic Church. He has performed ceremonies on the  beach, in parks, in gardens, at historical mansions, and more. He is the exception rather than the rule, but if you want a Catholic ceremony and one of you is divorced, then you have to find a church that will allow the ceremony to take place or a priest willing to perform the ceremony elsewhere.

If you and your spouse-to-be are of two different religions, choosing a venue to hold the wedding ceremony can be a challenge. For example, if one of you is Jewish and the other is not, a synagogue probably will not be willing to perform the wedding ceremony. Again, this forces you to make some decisions. The non-Jewish person can convert, or you have to find a way to incorporate the Jewish traditions into the wedding ceremony. Or, you could try to find a rabbi willing to perform a Jewish ceremony at a different venue and without both the bride and groom being Jewish.

Another easy way to overcome religious differences is to pick a neutral venue. Rather than choosing to have the ceremony in a religious institution, choose a non-religious location. This does not mean you have to sacrifice some of the religious traditions of the ceremony; it simply means you have to be flexible on the location of the ceremony venue.

Choosing the Officiant

The officiant is the person who performs the wedding ceremony. In some situations, such as ceremonies held in religious institutions, you might not have a choice in who performs the ceremony. Religious institutions often assign or have specific people in the institution for this task. Other institutions have several people who perform the ceremony, but it might depend on the date of the wedding or the availability of the officiant. If you have your heart set on a particular person officiating the wedding ceremony, you might have to adjust and choose the wedding ceremony date according to the officiant's availability. Whether you are able to choose your officiant, you and the groom should spend time getting to know him or her and giving the officiant an opportunity to get to know you individually and as a couple.

If you have the option to choose the officiant, choose carefully. You want to find someone whom you and your spouse-to-be can build a good rapport with. The officiant plays a pivotal role in the wedding ceremony. You want to choose someone you feel comfortable with and who will perform the ceremony in the manner you and your fiancé want.

CASE STUDY: IT IS OFFICIAL WITH THE RIGHT OFFICIANT

Rev. Laura C. Cannon
Divine Transformation, LLC.
4925 Lee Farm Ct.
Ellicott City, MD 21043
443-562-4709
RevLaura@divinetransformation.com
www.divinetransformation.com

Reverend Laura Cannon, a wedding officiant from Divine Transformation, has officiated approximately 200 second weddings. According to Cannon, in many cases the bride and groom are both getting remarried. Among those where one partner is walking down the aisle for the first time, it is an even split between the men and women.

Typically, the style of the wedding ceremony is the opposite of whatever their first wedding experience was. The second wedding focuses more on the couple and less on the "hoopla" surrounding the wedding. Cannon says she sees more nontraditional settings for second nuptials, such as a private residence, bed and breakfast, local venues, and restaurants with private rooms. In her experience, second weddings often have more of a family vibe, as well as the presence of children from previous marriages.

Cannon involves the children by having them take the place of the traditional bridal party. At the couple's stage in life, it is not their friends who need to stand up and support their decision; it is their children. The reverend also involves the children by having the parents and children take vows with each other. The children (biological and step) make vows to their parent and about-to-be stepparent to support their marriage and their new family. The parents then promise to make a home for their children and new family where all feel supported and included. Candle lighting and sand ceremonies, where the kids come up and participate, are also very popular ways to include the children in the second wedding ceremony.

Identifying the Items You Need to Buy or Rent

Once you have the ceremony venue booked, or even when you are still evaluating the venue, you should assess the items you need to rent or buy for the ceremony. One of the first things to obtain from the ceremony venue is the rules and regulations packet, and the packet that describes what the rental fee for the ceremony venue includes. From this information, you can determine which items you need to rent or buy to pull off the wedding ceremony.

For example, assume you chose a botanical garden for the wedding ceremony. Although a botanical garden might not require a bunch of decorations, especially flower décor, you will have to rent chairs, assemble some sort of an altar, **chuppah**, or other location for the officiant, bride, and groom to stand. You also might have to create an aisle by renting or buying an aisle runner.

Items you may need to buy or rent include:

- Chairs (for an outside wedding or alternative to a church)
- Aisle runner
- Flower decorations (altar, pew, chair)
- Altar, gazebo, or chuppah (for outside weddings or alternative locations to religious buildings)
- Tent
- Unity and taper candles
- Matches or lighter
- Guest book and pen

Vows

With all of the hoopla that goes into planning a wedding, it is easy to forget that the most important part of the wedding ceremony is the vows. The wedding vows are the true meaning of the wedding ceremony. You may choose to use pre-written or traditional vows, or you may choose to write your own vows.

Traditional

Traditional vows typically fall under a religion. Here are some samples of traditional vows you can use in your second wedding ceremony. You can use the vows as is, or you can work with your wedding officiant to alter the vows to fit your needs.

Protestant vows

I, _____, take thee, _____, to be my wedded wife/husband, to have and to hold from this day forward, for better, for worse, for richer, for poorer, in sickness and in health, to love and to cherish, 'til death do us part, according to God's holy ordinance; and thereto I pledge thee my faith [or] pledge myself to you [or] plight thee my troth.

Lutheran vows

I, _____, take you, _____, to be my husband/wife, and these things I promise you: I will be faithful to you and honest with you; I will respect, trust, help, and care for you; I will share my life with you; I will forgive you as we have been forgiven; and I will try with you better to understand ourselves, the world, and God through the best and the worst of what is to come, as long as we live.

Episcopal vows

I vow to be your faithful wife/husband, understanding that marriage is a lifelong union and not to be entered into lightly, for the purpose of mutual fellowship, encouragement, and understanding; for the procreation of children and their physical and spiritual nurture. I hereby give myself to you in this cause with my sacred vow before God. In the name of God, I, _____ take you, _____, to be my wife/ husband, to have and to hold from this day forward, for better, for worse, for richer, for poorer, in sickness and health, to love and to cherish, until we are parted by death. This is my solemn vow.

Methodist vows

Will you have this woman/man to be your wife/husband to live together in holy marriage? Will you love her/him, comfort her/him, honor and keep her/him in sickness and in health, and forsaking all others, be faithful to her/ him, as long as you both shall live?

In the name of God, I, _____, take you, _____, to be my wife/ husband, to have and to hold from this day forward, for better, for worse, for richer, for poorer, in sickness and in health, to love and to cherish until we are parted by death. This is my solemn vow.

Presbyterian vows

I, _____, take thee, _____, to be my wedded wife/husband, and I do promise and covenant, before God and these witnesses, to be your loving and faithful husband/wife, in plenty and in want, in joy and in sorrow, in sickness and in health, as long as we both shall live.

Baptist vows

Will you, _____, have _____ to be your wife/husband? Will you love her/him, comfort and keep her/him? And forsaking all others, remain true to her/him, as long as you both shall live?

I, _____, take thee, _____, to be my wife/husband, and before God and these witnesses I promise to be a faithful and true wife/husband.

Roman Catholic vows

I, _____, take you, _____, to be my wife/husband. I promise to be true to you in good times and in bad, in sickness and in health. I will love you and honor you all the days of my life.

I, _____, take you, _____ for my lawful wife/husband, to have and to hold from this day forward, for better, for worse, for richer, for poorer, in sickness and health, until death do us part.

Eastern Orthodox vows

Both bride and groom recite these vow silently. Consult with your church to follow the traditions.

Unitarian vows

I, _____, take you, _____, to be my wife/husband, to have and to hold from this day forward, for better, for worse, for richer, for poorer, in sickness and in health, to love and cherish always.

_____, will you take _____ to be your wife/husband; love, honor, and cherish her/him, now and forevermore?

Jewish vows

Traditional Jewish ceremonies do not have an actual exchange of vows; it is implicit in the ritual. However, many Reform and Conservative ceremonies state the following:

"Do you, _____, take _____ to be your wife/husband, promising to cherish and protect her/him, whether in good fortune or in adversity, and to seek together with her/him a life hallowed by the faith of Israel?"

Writing your own vows

You also have the option of writing your own vows. Especially because it is a second wedding, writing your own wedding vows might allow you to express the true meaning of this marriage to you. Although this might hold true for a first wedding as well, those who have been married before tend to learn lessons from their first marriage that can positively affect the second marriage. The challenge is that you might have a million ideas swimming through your mind, but when you sit down to put pen to paper, it can be difficult to express how you truly feel. In addition, when you write your own vows, you have to memorize and recite the vows on your own without any prompts from the officiant.

If you are stuck, or just need a little inspiration, here are some vow-writing prompts to get you started.

- I knew I wanted to spend the rest of my life with you when…
- The top ten reasons why I love you are…
- When I envision our life 30 years from now, I…
- When I look into your eyes, I see…
- When you touch me, I…
- I knew I fell in love with you when…
- When you look at me, I…
- Before you came into my life, I…

You can also answer these questions to help you put your vows together:

- How did you first meet?
- What were your first impressions?
- When did you first realize you were in love?
- What do you love the most about your future spouse?
- What was the most romantic moment in your relationship?
- What are you most looking forward to in your marriage?

Vows with children

For a second wedding, when there are children involved, many couples choose to recite vows to the children as well. After the bride and groom recite their vows to each other, the bride and groom then say their vows to all of the children. This is a touching way to include the children in the ceremony and to allow the children to be a part of the ceremony. Some couples even exchange a special family medallion, necklace, or bracelet with each of the children as part of the family wedding vows.

Sample vows:

Groom: "(State the name of the child or the names of the children), I want you to know that I as I marry your mother, I am not only marrying her, but I also am marrying you as well. You are a part of the bond and relationship that your mother and I share, and I want to continue to share the love I feel for her with you.

I promise to be fair, honest, and available for you as I am for your mom. I promise to earn your love, respect, and friendship. I will not attempt to replace your father, but I hope you will make a special place in your heart(s) for me, as I will do for you. On this day when I marry your mom, I marry you, and I promise to love and support you as my own."

Bride: "(State the name of the child or the names of the children), I want you to know that as I marry your father, I am not only marrying him, but I also am marrying you as well. You are a part of the bond and relationship that your father and I share, and I want to continue to share the love I feel for him with you.

I promise to be fair, honest, and available for you as I am for your dad. I promise to earn your love, respect, and friendship. I will not attempt to replace your mother, but I hope you will make a special place in your heart(s) for me, as I will do for you. On this day when I marry your dad, I marry you, and I promise to love and support you as my own."

The bride and groom's children then responded to the following vows when read by the pastor:

(Children's names), do you promise to love your mother and her new husband?

Children respond: "I do."

Do you promise to support their marriage and your new family?

Children respond: "I do."

Do you promise to accept the responsibility of being their children, and to encourage them, support them, and accept them just as our heavenly Father accepts us?

Children respond: "I do."

(Children' names), do you promise to love your father and his new wife?

Children respond: "I do."

Do you promise to support their marriage and your new family?

Children respond: "I do."

Do you promise to accept the responsibility of being their children, and to encourage them, support them, and accept them just as our heavenly Father accepts us?

Children respond: "I do."

The wedding ceremony is one of the most important and meaningful parts of the wedding. The ceremony is the portion of the wedding that binds you as husband and wife, and connects your two separate families into one. When you take the planning of your ceremony step-by-step, it ensures you remember of all of the details and make your second wedding as special as you want it to be.

Money-Saving Tips for Choosing a Location

Money-saving tip #1: Contact your local historical society to ask if any of your area's mansions are available for a wedding ceremony or reception. You could hold the festivities either indoors or outside if the home has gardens. Frequently, they are available for a reasonable fee given as a donation to the historical society.

Money-saving tip #2: When you speak with the historical society, ask for recommendations on free wedding locations. Its staff members know your locality well and may be able to direct you to the perfect place.

Money-saving tip #3: You or your fiancé's alma mater's banquet hall is another great place to consider. As an alumna or alumnus of the school, you may find you have access to university locales at a terrific price. Ask your alumni organization or office for a contact.

Money-saving tip #4: Were you or your fiancé in the military? If so, a military chapel is another consideration. As a veteran, you may find a great deal.

Money-saving tip #5: If your family or friends have a vacation home on the lake or ocean, in the mountains, or in another beautiful spot, find out if you can use it for your ceremony and your reception. One word of caution: Make sure any rental equipment you need to pay for does not end up costing more than a venue with everything you need included in its price.

Money-saving tip #6: Waterfront wedding ceremonies are still one of the most romantic locations. Although you will have to pay for a license, it will be nominal.

Money-saving tip #7: Do you live near an arboretum? For autumn, spring, and summer weddings, you will not be disappointed in the view. Plus, the price may be exactly right.

The second most important aspect of the wedding is the party that follows the ceremony: the reception. After all, you want to share your happiness with everyone that has just witnessed the joining of the two of you into one. *Chapter 8 goes into the details you need to know to plan the best wedding reception ever — the celebration, the party, and the festivities.*

CHAPTER EIGHT

The Celebration

You have organized your plan of attack. You have an overall view and a detailed view of what it takes to plan a second wedding. Now, it is time to get into the details of planning the wedding reception, the party after the ceremony. In other words, it is time to party! This chapter covers how to choose a venue or location for the reception. It also helps you evaluate the items the venue does not provide that you might need to rent or buy. Finally, it discusses planning the menu — be it just serving champagne and cake or appetizers to a full-course meal. This chapter covers the overarching strategy of finding, interviewing, and hiring vendors. It will provide an overview of the types of vendors you may need to hire for the wedding ceremony and reception — the professionals that will help you turn the venue into a real party or celebration.

Choosing the Reception Venue

The reception venue is where the celebration really begins. It is the foundation on which to build all of the details and other aspects of putting the party together. The reception allows you and your guests to celebrate the joining of your two families. The reception could reflect the same style you had for your ceremony, or it could be the direct opposite. That might sound confusing, but if you choose to have a small and intimate wedding ceremony just the two of you and your witnesses, then you might wish to throw a big party to which you can invite everyone else to celebrate your big day. You also might choose to carry the small and intimate theme of the wedding ceremony to the reception.

Questions to ask your reception venue

When you visit various reception venues, be sure to bring a list of questions with you. Being informed is one of the best methods of staying on top of any hidden costs, stresses, or other issues that a locale could cause.

- Is it available on your wedding date? If not, is it available on any of your backup dates?

- Are there a set number of hours you will have access to the venue? If you run over, are there additional fees? If so, what additional fees you are responsible for paying?

- What is the structure of its costs? Flat fee per head, by the hour, or a combination of these costs?

- Do you have to use its in-house caterer, or can you hire your own?

- Are there fees associated with either scenario? For example, some venues have a "corking fee," which is a fee for each bottle of wine or champagne they pop open at your wedding reception, whether the guests drink the entire bottle or not.

- Does the venue have a liquor license? Must you purchase from its bar, or can you supply the alcohol for your reception? Some venues allow you to supply the alcohol, which means you can buy it wholesale and save money on the cost of the liquor. In this case, you just might need to hire bartenders to serve the drinks to your wedding guests. If you go this route, do not forget drink mixers and garnishments you might need that the venue does not supply.

- Ask where the buffet is set up and other logistic questions. If possible, try to visit the location when it is set up for a wedding reception. It is much easier for you to visualize what your own wedding will look like by seeing what the venue looks like when it is set up for another wedding. This provides you with ideas on what you like and what you do not like about the wedding setup so you can discuss your options with the venue coordinator.

- What is the staff-to-guest ratio? When the venue provides staff for your wedding, how many waiters, bartenders, and other staff people are assigned to you based on the number of guests you have at the wedding.

- What is provided? Remember, the more provided in the basic cost, the better for your budget. Some venues are a one-stop-shop, so you literally can obtain anything you need from them for your wedding — tables, chairs, linens, tableware, and more. Other venues are just that, the venue, which means that you are working with a blank slate that you have to fill with any of the items you need. In other words, you have to rent or buy all of the other items you need to pull off the wedding.

- Are there enough outlets for lighting, equipment, and audio requirements? When you hire a DJ or live band, have them come in and assess the venue for their needs as well. This ensures that the day of the wedding there is not a problem with your entertainment getting started or the chance of them blowing a fuse box and the whole place going dark.

- Is there a dance floor, or does one need to be brought in? If there is not a dance floor, can the venue arrange to have one brought in? Is there an additional fee? How big a dance floor do you need to accommodate the number of guests you have coming to the wedding? Where will the dance floor fit?

- Are there restrictions on decorations, dress code, or music?

- Are there enough restrooms for your number of guests? Are they clean? Is there a bathroom attendant assigned to the bathrooms or should you hire someone to take care of the wedding guests in the bathrooms?

- Will staff be on hand to keep them clean and stocked during the celebration?

- Is there enough parking, and is the entrance easy to access from the parking lot?

- Are any other wedding ceremonies and/or receptions going on at the same time as yours? On the same day? Is there any chance that you will have difficulty having the appropriate access to decorate and set up?

- Ask for references of past gatherings. If you can get them, this will be a valuable resource for you. Once you obtain the references, it is imperative that you check them. Previous brides and grooms can provide invaluable insight to the problems and issues that might arise that you are not even thinking about. They can help you avoid pitfalls that they were not able to avoid on their wedding days as it pertains to the specific venue.

- Will the manager be on hand throughout the entire event? Does he or she seem flexible and likeable? Is this the same person you have been working with to plan your wedding or somebody different? If it is somebody different, how will the person you have been working with ensure the person on duty has the proper information?

- Does the venue have liability insurance? If so, how much is the coverage amount?

Choosing the reception venue starts with the atmosphere. If you have a traditional wedding ceremony, carry the tradition to the receptions, which leads to venues such as hotel ballrooms, historic mansions, and religious institutions. If you are lucky, you even might be able to rent one venue for both the ceremony and the reception.

The second major factor to consider when choosing a venue is the size. Make sure the reception venue holds the number of wedding guests you intend to invite. For example, you might need a larger reception venue if you are planning a sit-down dinner for 200 guests than if you are planning a reception with heavy appetizers and cocktails, or a champagne and cake wedding.

Location Uses	Location Services
❏ Ceremony and reception	❏ Food Included with site
❏ Reception only	❏ No food, bring own/caterer
❏ Changing clothes	❏ Chairs/tables Included
❏ Dancing	❏ Rentals Required
❏ Other: _____	❏ Other: _____

Location Details	Location Features
❏ Can walk from ceremony	❏ Beautiful interiors
❏ Proximity to ceremony	❏ Near the water
❏ Indoors	❏ Under tent
❏ Outdoors	❏ Daylight features
❏ Indoor and outdoor	❏ Evening features
❏ Other: _____	❏ The view
	❏ Other: _____

Location Style	Location Special Requirements
❏ Antique/old-world	❏ Handicapped access
❏ Modern	❏ A coat check
❏ Formal	❏ Children's area
❏ Casual and intimate	❏ Parking
❏ Fun and jazzy	❏ Other: _____
❏ Other: _____	

Must accommodate:	Budget:

Identifying the Items You Need to Buy or Rent

When you are shopping for venues, it is fine to love the way the location looks, but it is also important to determine what comes with the venue. Some locations only rent out the space, so the rental fee you pay is simply a fee to use the property. This can be good or bad. It can be beneficial because you have a blank slate that you can turn into the wedding reception room of your dreams. It can be a disadvantage because it means that you will have to rent and buy many items to turn the room into what you want it to be, which affects your wedding budget.

Most hotel ballrooms, for example, offer you a choice of different packages. These packages cover a variety of categories, including tables and chairs, linens, food and beverages, a dance floor, and things of this nature. Other venues might offer their own packages as well. Look through the packages to ensure the venue is offering you what you want and need for the reception and to make a list of any of the items the venue does not offer, so you know what you need to rent or buy for the wedding reception.

Some of the items you might need to rent or buy include:

- Tables
- Chairs
- Linens (table covers, napkins, chair covers)
- Caterer
- Dance floor or platform flooring (such as under a tent for a wedding in the grass)
- Wait staff
- Bartender

- Bar
- Audio/visual equipment
- Decorations
- Table centerpieces
- Favors
- **Place cards** or seating chart
- Seating chart holder/frame
- Tent
- Heaters or misters (to heat or cool outside areas)

Planning the Menu

The menu, too, correlates with the style of the wedding reception you choose to throw. If you are serving a sit-down meal or a buffet, you have to choose each of the courses of the meal. If the venue offers catering, they typically will not allow you to bring in an outside caterer. This is, however, one of the details to find out. It might be easier for you to have the venue handle the catering as well, but bringing in your own caterer will allow you to offer the menu you want. This is especially true if you are having a vegan, vegetarian, or kosher wedding menu.

Have an idea if how many courses and what type of menu you have in mind before sitting down with the caterer. You should share this information with the caterer and then the caterer can tell you what options they can offer to meet your needs. The caterer also might be able to make suggestions on creating a menu that differentiates your wedding from your first wedding and the typical wedding. For example, instead of serving sorbet to clean the palette in between courses in a dish, the caterer might be able to serve the sorbet in mini-ice cream cones and offer guests the option to choose between two different flavors.

Types of menus include:

- Appetizers and cocktails only
- Sit-down served meal
- Buffet
- Champagne and cake only
- Some combination of these options

One misconception that many brides and grooms have is that a buffet-style wedding reception is less expensive than a served meal. This is not necessarily the case because you still have to hire people to staff the buffet. You might even have to pay for or rent the equipment to keep the food hot or cold while it is on the buffet. It is comparable in price to having the wait staff to serve the meal, so having a buffet does not necessarily put less of a dent in your budget.

Deciding Which Vendors You Need

When you have a venue and you know what services and items the venue offers, and then you can determine the vendors that you need to hire. Some of the vendors you might have to hire include:

- Caterer
- Linen company
- DJ/band/entertainment
- Glassware and tableware (plates and silverware)
- Tables and chairs
- Florist
- Decorator
- Baker
- Audio/visual company
- Tent rental company

Again, which vendors you have to hire depends on what the venue you have chosen provides. In special situations, you might have to consider other vendors. For example, if you are planning an outside wedding and a cold front arrives during the week of your wedding, you will need to rent outside heaters from a party rental company.

Finding vendors

Wedding vendors are plentiful. The key is finding the right vendors for the wedding you are trying to plan, along with reputable vendors you can trust to show up and do their jobs on the day of your wedding. Fortunately, you can find wedding vendors several ways:

- Ask people you know who have recently been married.
- Ask the venue for their preferred vendor list.
- Attend bridal shows.
- Look them up in the phone book.
- Check out review sites.
- Go to the forums on wedding websites to seek referrals from other brides in your area.
- Put a call out for referrals on your social media pages.

Once you have a list of potential vendors, your work is just beginning. Contact each vendor on your list. The first question to ask them is if they are available on the day and time of your wedding. If they are not, then move on to the next vendor in that category. You even might ask the vendor if they would recommend one of their competitors/colleagues for the job. If the vendor is available for your wedding date and time, then schedule an appointment to meet face-to-face.

How to interview vendors

When you show up for the meeting with the vendor, come prepared. Bring along your wedding notebook or organizational system, so you can show the vendor what you are looking for to ensure they are able to provide you what you want. Next, ask to see their portfolio of work. Whether it is a band, caterer, florist, or some other vendor, they should have an album of pictures, a video, or some form of presentation to illustrate their work.

Always ask for references for other clients they have worked with, and try to find clients that had a wedding similar to the one you are planning. Always, always, always check these references.

Ask each vendor a lot of questions. Make sure you get the answers to all of the questions you have. Many of the remaining chapters in this book provide you with specific interview questions for the specific type of vendor. Here, however, are some general questions to ask vendors, beyond those already presented:

1. How many events do you book for the same day?

2. Are you the person who will be performing the service, or will you be sending someone else? If it is someone else, when can you schedule a time when I can meet with that person?

3. How long have you been in business?

4. Describe a wedding that had an unexpected problem. What did you do to resolve it?

5. Have you ever worked at my venue before? If so, when and how often?

6. Do you work alone, or do you bring other staff with you? If you bring other staff, how many do you bring, and what jobs are they responsible for performing?

7. In an emergency, if you are not able to perform your service the day of my wedding, what is your backup plan?

Choosing the vendor that is right for you

In general, choosing the right vendor comes down to two factors. The first factor is that the vendor can provide you with what you need. The second primary factor for choosing a vendor is rapport. You will be working with your wedding vendors for months and at times up to a year or more. This means you need to be able to work with the vendor for an extended period.

Money-Saving Tips

Money-saving tip #1: Ignore high-profile ads for reception halls. These places are unlikely to offer any savings, as they are considered prime reception locations.

Money-saving tip #2: To avoid high-priced rental fees, focus your attention on reception halls that already have tables, chairs, linens, and other equipment included in their cost.

Money-saving tip #3: Comparison shop in every step of your planning. Keep notes on what you see, what your impressions are, and any other bit of information you learn about the establishment.

Money-saving tip #4: Unless your heart is completely set on crystal, ultra-fine linens, and other pricey extras, take some time to look at smaller banquet halls. Often, their prices are much more reasonable. You may have to trim your guest list, but that will give you increased savings elsewhere.

Money-saving tip #5: If you do choose a home reception or another location that will require you to rent equipment, keep accurate lists so when you begin comparing prices, you know exactly what you need.

Money-saving tip #6: Although an outdoor location is a beautiful option, do not forget that if the weather does not cooperate, you will need an alternate location. Some venues offer both outdoor and indoor locales for the same price; check into this, as it will save you money, time, and stress.

Planning a wedding has numerous intricate details. Two of the biggest challenges are getting your ceremony location and your reception location identified and booked. Once you have the location or locations booked, it is time to fill in the details, such as hiring the rest of the vendors you need to complete the wedding. *Chapter 9 provides you with tips, advice, and help on choosing your wedding invitations and other stationery.*

Invitations and Wedding Stationery

Invitations are the first impression of your wedding, so many brides and grooms put a lot of time and thought into choosing the look and feel of the invitation and its wording. As you are gathering information on the type of vendors you need to hire and gathering contact information on the ones you want to meet, you can start shopping for and putting

together your wedding invitations and other stationery. This chapter covers everything there is to consider about the wedding invitations, including the style of invitations and how the wording on the invitations should differ for a second wedding. The chapter also discusses the other wedding stationery, such as response cards, maps/directions and thank-you cards that are ordered with the invitations.

Because it is a second wedding, this chapter also offers alternatives to the traditional invitation and response system, including a checklist of the stationery items to consider. In addition, the chapter explains your options for planning the seating arrangements, including mixing guests from each family so they can get to know each other, but also paying special attention not to sit guests that do not get along near each other. Finally, the chapter offers information on e-invitations as an alternative to paper invitations, how to manage responses, and ways you can save money in the invitation and stationery area of the budget.

Wedding Invitations

Wedding invitations are a key element to the wedding because they are the first impression of your wedding style, tone, and formality. The style or design of the wedding invitation you choose should match the formality and style of the wedding you have planned. For example, if you are having a formal wedding in a religious institution and expect formal attire at the reception, then your invitations and other wedding stationery should send this message. If you are having a beach wedding, where you are standing in the sand wearing flip flops or no shoes at all, with a clambake reception to follow, your invitations should reflect this with a more laid-back or even beach theme.

Wedding invitation wording

One of the primary differences on the wedding invitations for a second wedding is the wording. Generally, when it is a second wedding for both the bride and groom, the bride and groom host the wedding. The wedding invitations reflect this with wording such as:

> *Jane Ann Bride*
>
> *and*
>
> *Joseph Phillip Groom*
>
> *Cordially invite you to...*

The wording for the invitations might vary according to the situation. If it is the first wedding for the bride and the parents are paying for the wedding, then traditional wording could be used. If both parents are chipping in, or the couple wants to honor both sets of parents, no matter who is paying, then invitation wording can reflect this as well.

You are hosting the wedding:	
Sample 1 (formal)	**Sample 2 (informal)**
Together with their parents, Julia Esabella Sanmeters and Nicholas Kristoff Demett request the honour of your presence at their marriage on Sunday, the fourth of March Two thousand and twelve at six o'clock in the evening Mount Zion Church 11890 Leaf Avenue Chicago, Illinois	Mary Stevens & Chuck Henderson have chosen the first day of their new life together as June 20, 2012. You are invited to share in their joy as they exchange marriage vows at 4:00 p.m. at Church by the Sea 19 Riverside Drive Sand Key, FL
The bride's parents are hosting the wedding:	
Sample 1 (formal)	**Sample 2 (formal)**
Mr. and Mrs. Oliver Durand request the honour of your presence at the marriage of their daughter Sophie Lynn Durand to Jeffrey Luke Lautrec son of Mr. and Mrs. Michael Lautrec Saturday, the third of March Two thousand and twelve at two o'clock in the afternoon Fox Green Country Club 2621 Hunter Avenue Atlanta, Georgia	Mr. and Mrs. Oliver Durand request the honor of the presence of _____ at the marriage of their daughter Sophie Lynn to Mr. Tim Montgomery on Saturday, the twenty-fourth of March Two thousand and twelve at two o'clock in the afternoon Fox Green Country Club 2621 Hunter Avenue Atlanta, Georgia

Both sets of parents are hosting the wedding:

Sample 1 (formal)	Sample 2 (formal)
Mr. and Mrs. Tomas Kling and Mr. and Mrs. Frederick Langston invite you to share in the joy of the marriage uniting their children Ashley Marie and Patrick Everett on Saturday, the eighth of April at eleven o'clock in the morning San Bay Yacht Club 42 Burgundy Drive Los Angeles, California	Mr. and Mrs. Rick White and Mr. and Mrs. Tim Burrough request the honor of your presence at the marriage of their children Sharon Lynn White and Todd Michael Burrough as they happily unite their hearts, their lives and their cultures through marriage on Saturday, the twenty-fourth of November Two thousand and twelve at six o'clock in the evening The Cross Community Church

The groom's parents are hosting the wedding:

Sample 1 (formal)	Sample 2 (formal)
Mr. and Mrs. Michael Edward Sanchez request the honour of your presence at the marriage of Linh Thu Quy Do to their son Nathan Michael Sanchez on Saturday, the seventh of July two thousand and twelve at half past five o'clock in the evening The Houstonian Hotel, Club and Spa 111 North Post Oak Lane Houston, Texas Reception immediately following	As we shall become one to share all the days of our lives... Mr. and Mrs. Feeney request the honor of your presence at the marriage of their son Lucas Feeney to Patricia Brooks on the fifth of December two thousand twelve at five o'clock in the evening Biltmore Resort 19 Biltmore Road Bellaire, Louisiana

E-invitations

A great debate exists as to whether wedding invitations should come into the modern world, in which an electronic wedding invitation is sent instead if a paper one. Sending your wedding invitations online can save you hundreds of dollars. Sending electronic wedding invitations also helps to save the environment because it saves the trees for the paper, gas emissions for the mailman to deliver them, postage for mailing out the invitations, and the postage for guests returning their response card to you.

E-invitation programs also have built-in RSVP options. When the wedding guest receives the electronic wedding invitation, it includes a link or an option for the guest to provide all of the information online that the guest normally would have to provide on a response card. Even if you choose to send out traditional hard-copy version of your wedding invitation, you can still use an online system to keep track of the RSVPS.

Using e-invitations also has its drawbacks. For one, it takes away the physical invitation you and many wedding guests like to have as a keepsake. Skipping hard-copy invitations also takes some of the tradition out of the wedding ceremony because a wedding invitation is the first thing wedding guests receive to set the tone for your wedding. In addition, you might be dealing with a crowd that is not computer savvy. Although it is rare, some of your guests might not have an email address to send the invitation. This means you have to send the e-invitation to someone else to pass it along to the guest or come up with a different way to invite these people to the wedding.

Reception Cards

Reception cards are also part of the wedding stationery when the wedding ceremony and the wedding reception are in two different locations. The reception card typically includes the name, address, and time of the wedding reception.

Sample reception verses:
The celebration continues with a Reception Luncheon for Julia Esabella Sanmeters and Nicholas Kristoff Demett at seven thirty in the evening European Crystal Banquet & Conference Center 519 W. Algonquin Road Arlington Heights, IL 60005
Dinner Reception to be held following ceremony at the Sheraton Sand Key Resort 1160 Gulf Boulevard Clearwater Beach, FL 33767
Reception, Dinner, and Dance immediately following ceremony Georgian Terrace Hotel 659 Peachtree Street NE Atlanta GA 30308

Response Cards

Response cards are included in the invitation envelope. This is the card and small envelope that the guests return to you or the hosts of the wedding to let them know if they will be attending or not. If they are attending, the response card also includes how many guests will be joining them, the names of each guest, and maybe even the dinner choice for each guest. You also may use a postcard-style response card.

It is a rule of etiquette for the response envelope to be pre-addressed to the person who needs to receive the response card. It is also a rule of etiquette for the envelope to have a stamp so the guest does not have to stamp the envelope to mail it. You also might offer guests the option of RSVPing electronically. They can either send the response information to an email address you put on the response card, or there are online services you can pay for to receive your own wedding RSVP URL. The company then tallies and calculates all of the response information on your behalf.

Response card wording

Sample 1	Sample 2
The courtesy of a reply is requested by the twentieth of August M _____ Please indicate number of each Chicken ___ Fish ___ Beef ___	Please reply by March 20th ( ) accept ( ) decline Name and meal choice (beef, chicken, vegetarian) M _____ Choice: _____ M _____ (date) Choice: _____

Directions/Maps

You may want to include a directions and map card inside of the wedding invitation envelope as well. This card can provide directions to the ceremony location. If the reception location is different, then the card should also contain directions from the ceremony venue to the reception venue. Some couples also choose to include a map on the directions card, or as a separate piece of paper or card stock.

Thank-You Cards

When you are ordering your wedding invitations, you also can order matching thank-you cards. You have the option to have a preprinted thank-you message on the front and inside of the thank-you cards. It is best to leave the inside of the car blank, so you can personalize your message to each guest. You also want to mention the gift they gave you.

Examples of thank-you card wording

Dear Uncle Elmer and Aunt Clara, Thank you for the lovely crystal vase. We will think of you every time we bring home beautiful, fresh-cut flowers.
Dear Colin and Susan, It was lovely to see you at our wedding. Thank you for sharing in our special day. Thank you, as well, for such a generous gift. We plan to use it to help purchase the teapot from our china collection.

> Dear Ben, Allison, and Courtney,
>
> Thank you for attending our wedding. It was such a beautiful and special day, and we are so grateful that you were there to share it with us!

Place Cards or Seating Chart

Seating arrangements are another decision to make during the time you are evaluating your other wedding stationery. Place cards have the name of the wedding guest and the table number they are assigned to printed on the card. A seating chart is printed on a large framed scroll or parchment paper for guests to look at as they enter the dining area. The seating chart is written in alphabetical

order by the guests' name and the table number they are assigned. The invitation vendor should sell place cards that match the rest of your invitation stationery, but you will have to print the seating information, or hire someone to print the seating information on the cards, once you have all of the RSVPs in and have arranged seating.

Planning the seating arrangements

One of the trickiest parts of planning a second wedding is planning the seating arrangements. You might want to mix and mingle the two different families at tables, so they have an opportunity to get  to know each other better. The hitch with a second wedding is that you also might have invited guests who do not get along with one another. An old family dispute between two of your aunts might require you to sit one aunt and uncle on one side of the room and the other aunt and uncle at a table on the other side of the room.

If one or both of you are planning to invite your ex-spouses, then the seating arrangements also can get a little hairy. If your parents despise your ex-spouse, you need to be cognizant of this when you are placing people at tables.

Because seating arrangements can change numerous times up to the wedding, use a system that is easy to change. Some couples use a drawing layout of the reception room that usually can be obtained from the venue. They use a pencil to write in the names of weddings guests as RSVPs come in. Once the seating arrangements are final, you type up a list of the names and table numbers that should be printed on each place card or the seating chart for the person creating these for you.

Money-Saving Tips

Money-saving tip #1: If your ceremony location and reception location are the same, you do not need to order separate reception cards. Simply print a line at the bottom of the wedding invitation that says something similar to "Reception to immediately follow."

Money-saving tip #2: It is cheaper to order all your wedding stationery at the same time rather than ordering it here and there.

Money-saving tip #3: Order more invitations and accessories than you need to account for mistakes or guests you forgot to include on your original guest list. It is less expensive to order extra stationery up front, than it is to place a reorder.

Money-saving tip #4: When determining the number of invitations and other stationery you need, remember you only need one set per address. For example, your guest list might be 200 people, but a lot of these are couples and families.

Money-saving tip #5: Cut out the expense of place cards or a seating chart by having open seating at the reception. This allows your wedding guests to choose where they want to sit and ensures guests who do not get along do not end up sitting next to each other.

Money-saving tip #6: Shop and compare several different local invitation stores, online retailers, and discount retailers. Go to a local invitation or stationery store to touch and feel the invitations. Once you find the one you want, see if an online retailer offers the same option at a less expensive price.

Money-saving tip #7: Put your crafty and design talented friends and family members to work. If your cousin is a graphic designer, hire him or her to design the invitation and accessories you want at a discounted rate and then work with a printer to print the designed materials for you. If you have a friend who has nice handwriting or knows calligraphy, have him or her help you address the invitations and create the place cards or seating chart. Use a pretty font that matches the wedding stationery to address the envelopes and print your own place cards. If you print your items, calculate the time it will take you as part of your costs.

The wedding invitation is an important aspect of the wedding because it announces the date, time, and place of your wedding and beckons your guests to participate in your big day. The wedding invitations for a second wedding do not necessarily have to be different from that of a first wedding. The primary and most common difference is that second wedding invitations typically have different verse or wedding invitation wording than a first wedding because in a second wedding, it is common for the bride and groom to host the event rather than their parents.

With the wedding invitations marked off your checklist, you now know how to let your guests know about your wedding. However, with all of your friends and family preparing to attend your big day, you still have plenty of planning details left on your checklist. It is time to start thinking about the flowers and decorations. *Chapter 10 provides insight into the meaning of flowers, how to choose the flowers for your bouquet, and flower decorations for the wedding ceremony and reception.*

CHAPTER TEN

The Blooms

Flowers have played a role in
the wedding ceremony all the
way back to ancient times.
Not only do the flowers act
as décor for the wedding
ceremony location and the
reception venue, but some
brides also choose flowers
for the meanings the flowers
hold. In this chapter, you
will learn everything you
need to know about flowers,
including information on

choosing ceremony and reception flowers as well as ways to save money on
the flowers you need and want for your wedding. The chapter also provides
the details on how to find, interview, and choose the right florist for the type
of wedding you are planning.

Before getting into the details of each of the flowers, first review the checklist
of possible areas where you might need flowers. Decide the flower bouquets,
decorations, and **boutonnieres** you will need for your wedding, and then
you can determine which types of flowers you want for each.

Flowers to order

Females	Males
❑ Bridal bouquet	❑ Groom boutonniere
❑ Maid of honor bouquet	❑ Best man boutonniere
❑ Bridesmaids bouquets	❑ Groomsmen boutonnieres
❑ Junior bridesmaids bouquets	❑ Ushers boutonnieres
❑ Flower girl petals	❑ Ring bearer boutonniere
❑ Mother of the bride corsage	❑ Father of the bride boutonniere
❑ Mother of the groom corsage	❑ Father of the groom boutonniere
❑ Grandmother corsages	❑ Grandfather boutonnieres
❑ Great-grandmother corsages	❑ Great-grandfather boutonnieres
❑ Godmother corsages	❑ Godfather boutonnieres
❑ Other corsages (attendants, readers, musicians)	❑ Other boutonnieres (attendants, readers, musicians)
❑ Other _____	❑ Other _____

Service/Reception Decorations	
❑ Altar decorations	❑ Place-card table flowers
❑ Aisle decorations	❑ Guestbook table flowers
❑ Chair decorations	❑ Gift table flowers
❑ Table centerpieces	❑ Food table flowers
❑ Head table centerpiece	❑ Bar flower arrangements
❑ Cake flowers	❑ Other decorations
❑ Cake table flowers	❑ Other _____
❑ Other _____	❑ Other _____

Choosing Bouquets

The primary bouquet you tend to focus your efforts on is the **bride's bouquet**. Several bouquet styles exist from which to choose. Bride bouquet styles include:

- **Hand-tied:** A hand-tied bouquet is just as it sounds. The stems of the flowers are all left in the open and the bouquet is tied, either with a ribbon or greenery.

- **Single blossom:** Some brides choose to carry a single flower with them down the aisle. This simplicity can be stunning.

- **Nosegays:** These are perfectly round bouquets, and even though they have been around for centuries, they are making a comeback in popularity. The size of the nosegay can range from small to large.

- **Arm bouquet:** This bouquet is triangular because you hold it in your hand and up to the crook of your arm. This is popularly seen by winners of beauty pageants but is also a good choice for a bridal bouquet.

- **Cascade:** A cascading bridal bouquet is often a large bouquet that includes greenery and flowers that taper off. These can be quite heavy, so it is important to consider you will be holding this bouquet for your photographs.

The style of the bridal bouquet you choose should coordinate with the style of your dress and the overall theme of your wedding. For example, a small intimate affair coordinates with a hand-tied bouquet, single blooms, or nosegays. Arm bouquets and cascade bouquets tend to be more elaborate, and therefore, tend to be for more formal weddings.

The bouquet style might dictate the types of flowers that work best for arrangements, so you should discuss this with your florist when choosing the style as well as the flowers you want to include in the bouquet. For example, single-bloom flowers tend to be flowers that have large blooms, and nosegays tend to be flowers that easily jut up against one another to create the round look.

Toss bouquet

The **toss bouquet** is typically a smaller version of the bride's bouquet to use during the reception tradition of tossing the bouquet. Bride's can use their actual bouquet, but most brides choose to have a toss bouquet especially created for the tossing ceremony.

> **Tip:** For some reason, many florists forget to bring the toss bouquet to the reception. If this happens, your wedding planner or someone you put in charge quickly can create a toss bouquet. You randomly can pull one flower from each of the table centerpieces, the bride's bouquet, and/or the bridesmaid bouquets to create a small toss bouquet. Use a rubber band to hold the stems of the flowers together and top it off with a ribbon bow. If ribbon is not available, then use the rubber band to tie up the flowers high on the stems so the flowers hide the rubber band.

Bridesmaid bouquets

When choosing bridesmaid bouquets, you can choose from the same styles that are available for bridal bouquets. It is common, however, for the bridesmaids' bouquets to be smaller than that of the bride. For example, if you want to carry a cascade bouquet and want your bridesmaids to carry cascades, then your bouquet should be a larger size.

Some brides choose a completely different style for the bridesmaids' bouquets. To match the bridesmaids' bouquets with the bride's, you might use the same color scheme but different types of flowers. Another option is to use the same flowers but use them in a different style.

Other bouquets or corsages

Traditionally, the mothers and grandmothers of the bride and groom have flowers, too. You might choose to create a small mini-bouquet for the mothers and/or grandmothers to carry with them as the escort takes them down the aisle. You also have the option of choosing a wrist or a pin-on corsage.

Flowers for the flower girl

The flower girl traditionally carries a basket of petals to drop down the aisle right before the bride enters. Check with your ceremony venue before

ordering flower petals, however. Not all venues allow this tradition, especially churches or religious institutions, because stepping on the flower petals can stain the carpet. If the church does not allow petals, you also have the option of using silk flower petals, which look just like real flower petals but will not leave marks on the carpet. The petals the flower girl traditionally drops are rose petals because the petals come in a variety of colors and are large. You could also have the flower girl walk with her basket or a small bouquet instead of dropping flower petals at all.

Boutonnieres

The boutonnieres are for the men in the bridal party and special family members. The groom's boutonniere is different in some way from the rest of the groomsmen's boutonnieres. For example, if you choose a white calla lily for the boutonnieres, the groom's boutonniere might include a small strip of palm folded over as the background for the lily, while all of the groomsmen simply have the flower.

Fathers and grandfathers of the bride and groom also receive boutonnieres. Ushers and male readers also may have a boutonniere. Women readers typically have a wrist or pin-on corsage.

CASE STUDY: FLOWERS WITH STYLE

WildFlowers Inc.
Beth LeonGuerrero
132 Towering Pine Drive
Summerville, SC 29456
843-367-8681
beth@wildflowersinc.com
www.wildflowersinc.com

Beth LeonGuerrero, owner of WildFlowers Inc. in South Carolina works with second time brides primarily planning small destination weddings. Often the ceremony is small and intimate with immediate family only. After the ceremony, the couple holds a party or celebration for friends and extended family.

Children from previous marriages tend to take part in planning the wedding, even one of the biggest parts of the wedding, the flowers. LeonGuerrero has had daughters even as young as preteens come to the floral consultation with their moms or future stepmoms. Girls love being a part of choosing wedding flowers and giving their input on their favorite colors and styles. The younger girls tend to steer the selections toward pinks, purple, and "bling" or "princess" themed designs. The older the daughters are more likely to influence the brides to choose things that are edgier or trendier. "Encore brides," as WildFlowers Inc. calls them, seem to care about the input of their daughters and future daughters and making them feel part of the decision and planning processes.

LeonGuerrero also has seen second time bride and grooms, with or without children, spend time crafting their own centerpieces. The DIY wedding trend is growing strong among all brides and grooms, first timers or otherwise, to stay budget friendly. The problem with DIY is the amount of time it takes to complete projects tends to be underestimated. DIY for your wedding décor, favors, invites, and more is extremely successful when you have children that can kick in some of the labor. Working on projects together serves dual purpose as bonding time for future step families, making them feel a part of the planning and saving money by contributing to the décor.

As a florist, LeonGuerrero embraces this trend and incorporates the DIY projects into the overall theme while providing the finishing touches and execution of the floral arrangements and decorations. Some of the most successful DIY décor projects LeonGuerrerol has seen in second weddings include families hanging lighting (string lighting, café lighting, and lanterns), potting plants for centerpieces and other decorations, painting vintage wood signs, and paper flowers used as bouquets, centerpieces, and more.

WidlFlowers Inc.'s "encore brides" tend to use venues such as beach houses, plantation homes, or similar venues. In these cases, flowers and other décor items, such as decorated arches and arbors, play a big role in defining the "altar" area. On several occasions, the second weddings were held at the couples' home. The couples in these cases spent some of their decorating budget into sprucing up their landscaping and décor by bringing in extra plants, both planted and potted, and ordering more blooming plants for the yard and house. Encore brides on a budget may use plants and/or standing floral arrangements for the altar area that also can be repurposed to the reception area. Flowers used as aisle markers also were repurposed to centerpieces or other table arrangements.

Second marriage brides and grooms tend to be less stressed, easier to please, and sometimes more fun to work with, according to LeonGuerrero. From a floral and design standpoint, she sees that second marriage couples very explicitly try to avoid repeating any of the elements of their first weddings. They absolutely do not want the same flowers, colors, vendors, style, or atmosphere of their first weddings. Because they are open to suggestions to maximize their budget, they may use flower-buying strategies that first time brides may not have the courage to consider. For example, LeonGuerrero had an encore bride hold an oyster roast/ barbeque as her reception. She gave the florist a budget and told her to do whatever flowers she wanted. LeonGuerrero cleaned the flower cooler out, so the bride got so much more for her money than if the florist had to special order flowers just to fit the bride's needs.

Altar Pieces and Ceremony Décor

Another common use of flowers in the wedding ceremony is as decoration for the wedding ceremony location. If you are marrying in a religious institution, the institution tends to have rules about whether or not you can have altar decorations, whether or not you can decorate the pews, and where you can include decorations in other parts of the building. Again, obtain this rule list from the venue before ordering any flower decorations.

Typical flower decorations for a ceremony include:

- Altar arrangement — typically one on each side of the altar
- For Jewish weddings — flowers for the chuppah
- Pew bows with flowers
- Flower arrangement at the guest book table
- Standing **candelabras** that line the aisle might have flowers or greenery to decorate each one
- Flowers for the bathrooms at the church or ceremony location
- Gazebo
- Chairs

When choosing flower decorations, it is common to choose the same or some of the same flowers for use in the bouquets and other areas of the wedding. In other words, the flowers and greenery you use should weave together all areas of the wedding.

Choosing Centerpieces

Each table at the reception should have a centerpiece. The styles of centerpieces from which you can choose truly run the gamut. Generally, the types of flower centerpieces you choose correlate with the overall style of the wedding. For example, a big formal wedding could have large candelabras with flowers and greenery decorating each one. A spring outdoor wedding might have a hand-tied bouquet of Gerbera daisies wrapped with ribbon and pinned with a pearl straight pin sitting in a round fish bowl vase.

Alternative centerpiece options do not have to include flowers at all. Some couples choose to weave a theme into their wedding, and they carry this theme into the centerpieces. For example, if the couple loves to travel, they could have each table represent a place they have been together. A frame holding a picture of the couple in the destination surrounded by symbols of the location would be the centerpiece instead of flowers.

Mirrors with various sized candles or votive candles are another alternative centerpiece. Not only does this cut down the cost of your flower budget, but these centerpieces also are easy to create and are easier to put to use after the wedding than flowers, which simply end up dying.

Reception Décor

Some of the other areas of the wedding reception you might want flowers for include:

- Cake or cake table
- Place card table
- Gift table
- Guest book table
- Bar(s)
- Bathrooms
- Buffet tables
- Food station tables
- Pool, lake, or pond for outdoor weddings
- Individual guest chairs

The venue you choose for your reception tends to dictate how much décor you need to buy or rent. For example, if you are having your ceremony and reception in a botanical garden, then the amount of flower decorations you need is probably zero. You still will need your bouquets and boutonnieres, however. Many hotel ballrooms are ornate enough that you do not necessarily have to add numerous decorations of your own, so you can choose which areas you want to decorate and which areas you can skip.

The Meaning of Flowers

For centuries, the flowers in a wedding have had a significance or meaning associated with them. In the first weddings, herbs, plants, and flowers were chosen to keep evil spirits away and represent special symbols in the wedding ceremony and reception. If you are a second bride that wants to choose meaningful flowers for the wedding, here are some of your options.

	Flower	Color	Meaning
Winter Flowers	Rose	White	Innocence
		Red	Love
		Yellow	Joy, friendship
		Peach	Appreciation, closing the deal, sincerity, gratitude
		Pink	Perfect, "I love you," grace, joy
		Dark pink	Thank you
		Crimson	Mourning
		Freesia	Innocence, friendship
	Holly		Domestic happiness, defense
	Poinsettias		Beautiful, purity
	Ivy		Wedding love, fidelity
	Amaryllis		Pride, beauty, determination
	Mistletoe		Affection
	Snowdrop		Hope, purity
	Iris		Faith, hope, wisdom, courage, admiration
Spring Flowers	Rose	White	Innocence
		Red	Love
		Yellow	Joy, friendship
		Peach	Appreciation, closing the deal, sincerity, gratitude
		Pink	Perfect, "I love you," grace, joy
		Dark pink	Thank you
		Crimson	Mourning
	Tulip	Red	Belief, powerful, declaration of love
		Yellow	Hopeless love
	Magnolia		Love of nature, nobility, perseverance
	Peonies		Happy life, happy marriage, compassion, bashfulness
	Daisies		Innocence, purity
	Hydrangea		Sincerity, vanity

	Flower	Color	Meaning
Spring Flowers continued	Lilac		First love, beauty, pride, youthful
	Daffodil		Unrequited love, chivalry
	Hyacinth	Blue	Constancy, sincerity
		Purple	Forgiveness
		Red/pink	Playful
		White	Lovely
	Heather	Lavender	Admiration, beauty, solitude
		White	Protection
	Carnation	Pink	"I'll never forget you"
		Red	"My heart aches for you"
		White	Innocence
		Yellow	Rejection
Summer Flowers	Stephanotis		Happiness in marriage
	Calla lilies	White	Purity, majestic beauty
	Lily of the Valley		Increased happiness, purity, sweetness
	Daisies		Innocence, purity
	Snapdragons		Graciousness
	Zinnia	Magenta	Lasting affection
		Scarlet	Constancy
		White	Goodness
		Yellow	Remembrance
		Orchids	Love, beauty
	Carnations	Pink	"I'll never forget you"
		Red	"My heart aches for you"
		White	Innocence
		Yellow	Rejection
	Heather	Lavender	Admiration, beauty, solitude
		White	Protection

Flower	Color	Meaning
Rose	White	Innocence
	Red	Love
	Yellow	Joy, friendship
	Peach	Appreciation, closing the deal, sincerity, gratitude
	Pink	Perfect, "I love you," grace, joy
	Dark pink	Thank you
	Crimson	Mourning
Sunflower		Adoration
Dahlias		Dignity, elegance
Aster		Variety, love, daintiness
Chrysanthemum	Red	"I love you"
	White	Truth
	Yellow	Sighted love
Morning glory		Affection
Freesia		Innocence, friendship

(Fall Flowers)

Finding a Florist

The fastest and easiest way to find a florist is a referral. If you are on your second marriage, you even might opt to use the same florist you did for your first wedding if you had a good experience the first time. If not, ask recently married couples whom they used for their flowers. Friends, family members, and coworkers are great starting points. Venue coordinators, such as your ceremony and reception locations, often work with various florists, so they might be able to provide you with a list of florists to interview.

Interview Questions for the Florist

Once you gather the list of florists you want to interview, call to schedule face-to-face meetings with each one. Your goal is to find a florist you feel comfortable with that also is capable of creating the floral pieces you want for your wedding. When interviewing your florists, here are some of the questions you should obtain answers to:

- Are you available on my wedding date?

- Do you have pictures of your work?

- How much experience do you have with weddings?

- Do you provide a delivery service?

- Will you deliver to more than one location?

- Is there a delivery fee?

- What are some quick thoughts you have for my wedding flowers?

- On average, how much does a complete set of wedding flowers cost?

- Can you provide flowers for a wedding the size of mine?

- What makes you a better choice than other florists?

- Can you obtain out-of-season or tropical flowers if needed?

- Do you provide setup for decorations?

- Do you offer any other rental services?

- What is your payment policy?

- What is your cancellation policy?

- Do you offer any special packages?

- Have you worked at my ceremony and/or reception location(s) before?

Money-Saving Tips

Money-saving tip #1: Move flower arrangements from the ceremony location to the reception location. For example, you might use altar arrangements to decorate the place-card table and the gift table.

Money-saving tip #2: Consider green plants and potted trees as alternative décor to flowers. You can rent or buy green plants and potted trees. Both types of greenery make great fillers to make a room that is too large feel cozy and comfortable. The greenery is also great cover for outlets, stains, and other unattractive areas in the room.

Money-saving tip #3: Choose flowers for your wedding that are in season. Seasonal flowers are less expensive than out-of-season flowers. If the florist has to order flowers that are out of season, you are going to pay a premium.

Money-saving tip #4: Find alternatives to flowers when you can. For example, replace flower centerpieces with theme centerpieces. Use greenery, such as ivy, to decorate candelabras, gazebos, chuppahs, and more to cut out or cut down on the number of flowers you have to buy.

Money-saving tip #5: Rent dried flower arrangements instead of using fresh flower arrangements. Some florists rent freeze-dried flower arrangements, which are less expensive than using fresh flowers that die anyway.

Whether you choose blooms that are meaningful or just aesthetically pleasing, you know what you need to need to look for in the flowers and the flower provider. Once you choose your flowers, it is now time to move on to another aspect of the wedding — the entertainment. The entertainment you choose can make or break the celebration — making it the best time your guests have had at a wedding or keep them sitting in their seats wondering when it is time to go home. *Chapter 11 covers entertainment options and how to choose the right entertainment for your wedding.*

CHAPTER ELEVEN

Let Us Entertain Them

A party is not a party without some major dancing tunes. While flowers play a starring role in the wedding ceremony and reception, its supporting role is the music incorporated into the celebration. In this chapter, you will find a few different options to entertain your guests and add ambiance to the ceremony and reception. You also will discover some tips on interviewing and hiring the right music vendor(s) for the wedding. A music checklist is included to make sure you have music and entertainment for the various times during the wedding you want to cover.

Music for the Ceremony

Ceremony music typically plays in the lobby or entrance of the ceremony location. This is typically background music while the guests take their seats and prepare for the ceremony to begin. If your budget permits, you could have live music, such as a harpist, trio, or quartet playing. An organist or pianist, especially in a religious institution is another option for ceremony music. Some brides even choose to have a singer or two perform. Finally, if the location has a sound system, you even can pipe in the background music through the system, in which case you only need someone to make the music changes when appropriate.

Music changes indicate to the wedding guests the different happenings that occur during the ceremony. While guests are being seated, background music plays, but the music changes when the mothers and grandmothers are seated. The music changes again as the bridal party walks down the aisle. The final music change is when it is time for the bride to walk down the aisle. During the ceremony, music may play in the background at certain points or be the focal point with a live performance. The bride and groom walk back down the aisle as husband and wife for the first time to their own song. The final music change signals to guests that they can file down the aisle after the bridal party.

If you are looking for classical music, traditional options for your ceremony include:

- "Bridal Chorus" from *Lohengrin* — Richard Wagner (You might recognize this as "Here Comes the Bride.")
- "Canon in D" — Johann Pachelbel
- "Air" — George Frideric Handel

- "The Prince of Denmark's March" — Jeremiah Clarke (also referred to as "Trumpet Voluntary in D Major")
- "Procession of Joy" — Hal Hopson
- "Trumpet Voluntary" — John Stanley
- "Trumpet Tune and Air" — Henry Purcell
- "Wedding March" — Mozart
- "Cantata No. 29" — Bach

DJ vs. Live Band

One of the great debates when hiring reception musicians is band or DJ? Generally, DJs are less expensive than bands, but bands tend to be more entertaining and engaging than DJs. Both have their own set of pros and cons. Some of the choice comes down to your own preference, but it also comes down to how much you want to spend on the music portion of your wedding.

Beyond price, brides and grooms cite the primary reason for hiring a DJ is their favorite songs can play exactly the way they love them. Bands, however, might not sound enough like the original musician. In addition, the band might not have the ability to play all of the songs that you want them to perform, while a DJ typically has a wide variety of music options or can easily obtain the song you want, if necessary.

In addition to playing the music, DJs and bandleaders often act as the master of ceremonies, or MC, for the wedding reception. The MC helps keep the reception moving according to schedule and ensures guests know what is happening. If the DJ or bandleader is acting as your MC, you want them to have the charisma, charm, and personality that gets guests up and dancing on the dance floor. If the MC or bandleader does not provide this service or does not have the personality to pull it off to your satisfaction, you can hire an MC, or if you hire a wedding planner, then he or she usually is able to fill this role as well.

iPod Your Wedding

Couples trying to save money and truly hear the songs by the original performers are also iPodding their weddings. Couples load their iPod with their favorite songs and in the order they want them to play at the reception. Connect the iPod to a docking station, speakers, and/or amp of the reception location, and pipe into the sound system of the room or area where the reception is taking place.

Using your iPod at your wedding is one of the least expensive ways to get the music and entertainment you want and need for your reception. You might have to rent the equipment, such as speakers and an amp, to make the music loud enough for the guests to hear it, if the location is not equipped for this option. You also might have to put someone in charge of stopping the iPod when announcements need to be made by the MC and restarting it again at the appropriate point. In addition, you will have the cost of hiring an MC, unless you are working with a wedding planner that can fill this role.

Interview Questions for the Entertainers

Finding the right musicians and entertainers for your wedding requires you to meet with them, interview them, and see sample performances of their work. Although you likely have a list of questions of your own, here are some questions to use as a starting point for interviewing a DJ or a live band.

Questions to ask prospective disc jockeys

When you have a list of disc jockeys you are interested in, be ready to ask them the following questions. This will help you save time and stress, as you will be able to narrow your selection of disc jockeys down with a few telephone calls.

- Do they specialize in a specific type of music? If so, find out what kind to be sure you are happy with the selection they will have. This could include swing, pop, rock, country, current hits, and oldies.

- Are they willing to play a variety of tunes? A little country, a little rock, or whatever you and your fiancé want?

- If you want certain songs played, but the disc jockey does not have them, will he or she pick them up? Or, as an alternate, will the disc jockey play your CDs or MP3s?

- Can you or your guests request songs during the reception? And, if the disc jockey has those songs, will he or she be willing to play them?

- Will the disc jockey be on his or her own, or is there an assistant or assistants that come and help? If there are, can you also meet them?

- Does the disc jockey have his or her own equipment, or do you or the reception venue need to supply it?

- How much room will the disc jockey need for equipment? Will a table be needed?

- When is setup? It is preferable if he or she is ready to go when the reception starts.

- What will he or she wear? If your wedding is formal and the disc jockey shows up in jeans and a T-shirt, this is something you will want to know ahead of time. If you have a preference, as in a tuxedo or suit for a man, ask if he will comply.

- What is the minimum amount of time the disc jockey will play?

- Will he or she take breaks? How many and how often?

- Ask about prices for the average length of a reception, four hours or so, and, if there is a range, ask what encompasses the difference in price.

- Is he or she willing to stay over if the reception runs longer than expected? If so, is there a charge for the extra time, and how much?

Questions to ask prospective bands

When you have a list of bands you are interested in, be ready to ask them the following questions. This will save you time when narrowing your selection.

- Do they have a signature sound or a specific type of music they specialize in? You want to know if they are into classics, rock, pop, country, or jazz, to name a few.

- Are they willing to play a variety of styles? This is especially important if you and your fiancé have drastically different tastes in music.

- If you have certain songs you want played, and the band is not familiar with them, are they able and willing to learn it for your reception? Do you need to supply the sheet music?

- Can you or your guests request songs during the reception? If they know the music, will they be willing to play these songs?

- How many members make up the band? Ask for their names, and ask if you can listen to them play. Also, find out if there are alternates that take the place of a member if one becomes ill.

- Will the band members bring their own equipment, or do you need to supply it? If you need to supply it, what do they need? Find out if your reception venue has these items.

- Do they prefer a stage, or are they all right without a stage as long as there is ample space? How much space do they need?

- When do they come to set up? It is preferable that they be ready to go when the reception starts.

- Do they dress casually, in suits, or tuxedos? If you have a preference to style of dress, will they comply?

- What is the minimum amount of time the band will play?

- Will they take breaks? How many and how often?

- Ask about their prices for the average length of a reception, four hours or so, and, if there is a range, ask what encompasses the difference in price.

- Are they willing to stay over if the reception runs longer than expected? If so, do they charge for the extra time, and how much?

Music Checklist

When you set up interviews with the music providers you are considering for your wedding, take copies of these comparison sheets along with you. As you discuss your needs and they go over the service packages they offer, takes notes directly on these sheets. You also can use the sheets as a guide to ask questions the provider does not give you up front, so you will have all of the information you need to compare the options you have properly.

Ceremony Musicians Comparison Chart	
Business name	
Contact person	
Address	
Telephone number	
Email address	
Fax number	
Website	
First impression	
Familiarity with your music	
Availability	

Ceremony Musicians Comparison Chart	
Rates	
Payment schedule and policy	
Cancellation policy	

Wedding Bands Comparison Chart	
Band name	
Contact person	
Address	
Telephone number	
Email address	
Fax number	
Website	
First impression	
Familiarity with your music	
Style of music	
Ability to learn new music	
Willingness to act as emcee	
Availability	
Rates	
Payment schedule and policy	
Cancellation policy	

DJ Comparison Chart

Company name	
Contact person	
Address	
Telephone number	
Email address	
Fax number	
Website	
First impression	
Familiarity with your music	
Style of music	
Willingness to get new music	
Willingness to act as emcee	
Availability	
Rates	
Special packages available	
Payment schedule and policy	
Cancellation policy	

Finalized Song List

Moment	Song	Artist
Before the processional		
Before the processional		
Before the processional		

Finalized Song List		
Moment	Song	Artist
The processional		
The bride's entrance		
During the ceremony		
During the ceremony		
During the ceremony		
The recessional		
Bridal party entrance to reception		
Bride and groom entrance		
First dance together		
Bridal party dance		
Mother and son dance		
Father and daughter dance		
Money dance		
Anniversary dance		
Cake cutting		
Bouquet toss		
Garter toss		
The final dance		
Other important songs		
Other important songs		

Finalized Song List		
Moment	Song	Artist
Other important songs		
Other important songs		
Other important songs		

Money-Saving Tips

Money-saving tip #1: Recycle musicians from the ceremony to the reception. For example, if you hire a harpist or string quartet for the ceremony, have them play during the cocktail hour of the wedding reception as well. Especially if the ceremony and reception are in the same location, you might be able to get a package deal for multiple hours over hiring the musicians for only one hour.

Money-saving tip #2: If you have talented musicians as family and friends, this is a good way to incorporate them into your wedding and obtain the entertainment you need. Ask your cousin to sing "Ave Maria" as your mothers are seated at the ceremony. Have your nephew who is a natural on the cello entertain guests as they sit at the ceremony and mingle during the cocktail hour. They are likely to do it without charging you, but you always can pay them a small thank-you fee or give them a special gift to show your appreciation.

Money-saving tip #3: Contact the music school of local high schools and colleges in your area. Typically, there are multitudes of hidden talent and garage bands that are just as good as hiring professional musicians. The difference is high school and college kids are looking to do it for experience or a few extra bucks, rather than the thousands of dollars you would spend on a professional band or musicians.

Money-saving tip #4: Cut down on the number of musicians in the band. If your heart is set on a live band, find out what the price difference is if you hire a five-piece band instead of seven-piece band. The fewer number of band members can save you money. Your other option is to cut the number of hours the band plays rather than cutting the number of band members. During the band breaks, you can pipe in background music or put your talented friends and family members to work.

Money-saving tip #5: Cut the band's playing time in half by having them start later or leave earlier. Fill in the blank time with a volunteer disc jockey from your group of friends or family.

Money-saving tip #6: If you and your fiancé are interested in having ethnic music played and your disc jockey does not have what you want, there is no need to purchase it. Check out your local library and rent it instead.

With all of your guests having a great time, dancing to the music, and laughing in their seats, you can let out a great big sigh of relief. You have managed to plan a fun and exciting time to celebrate your wedding day and provide a good time for everyone you know who wants to share this day with you. While your guests are being entertained, you want to capture all of these special moments, too. This way, you not only remember the fun you and they are having as it unfolds, but you also can look back at the good times for years to come. *Chapter 12 helps you work through the details of finding and hiring the photographer and videographer to preserve your wedding memories for years to come.*

CHAPTER TWELVE

You Ought to Be in Pictures

Every bride and groom reaches the celebrity status that lands them in the starring role of their own wedding pictures and wedding video. The photographer helps the bride and groom to preserve the wedding memories they are a part of, and even ones the bride and groom do not see during the wedding. In this chapter, you will discover how to find photographers that meet the style of photography you want. You also learn which questions to ask the photographers during the interview process. The chapter includes a wedding photo checklist to share with the photographer you hire to ensure you get all the shots you want. In addition to a photographer, you also might want to hire a videographer. The chapter covers how to find videographers that meet your style, questions to ask during the interview process, and a checklist of moments for recording. You also learn ways to save money on photographing and videotaping the wedding.

Choosing the Photographer

Finding a photographer can be easier than some of the other vendors because photographers have tangible samples of their work. You easily can see by looking at the sample photo books whether the photographer shoots the style of photography you are looking for your wedding. Start to assemble a list of possible photographers by obtaining referrals from friends, family members, and coworkers who recently have been married. You also might want to conduct some online research in wedding forums for your local area, where brides talk about the photographers they hired and what their experience with the photographer was.

One of the first things to look for in a potential photographer is that he or she shoots in the style you want. The three primary styles of photography include:

Traditional

This photography is the style that many are used to seeing. It consists of formal poses and group pictures. Couples tend to have this style as part of their wedding-day photographs, even if they have chosen to use another style for different aspects of their wedding day. For instance, a couple might want a more artistic approach to their wedding photos but also might want to have formal family pictures taken. Most wedding photographers, regardless of their style preference, are capable of staging and shooting a traditional, posed photograph.

Photojournalistic

The photojournalistic style captures all the moments of your wedding. It is more candid, and for this reason, is popular with couples. It tells your wedding story through photographs. The photographer aims to capture every meaningful moment, from the bride getting ready with her bridal party, to the final dance at the reception. A photographer who uses photojournalistic style is often creative. You will need to let down your guard a little, give him or her full control, and trust in the results. Remember to look at the photographer's portfolio before hiring him or her.

Artistic

The artistic style is used to describe photographers who are creative and use different lenses to garner different effects. They might do considerable work after the wedding to color in photos, using different enhancements. They likely will use a mix of traditional style and photojournalistic style.

Determining the style of photography you want helps you narrow down the options of photographers that provide the style you seek. Once you have your list assembled, you can schedule meetings to interview each photographer.

CASE STUDY: PICTURE THIS — SECOND WEDDINGS SET A DIFFERENT SCENE FROM FIRST WEDDINGS

Ambientimage Photography
Johanna Erin Jacobson
22728 Stagg Street
West Hills, CA 91304
310-795-6816 USA
(39) 339-88-27-165 Europe
johanna@ambientimage.com
www.ambientimage.com

Johanna Erin Jacobson from Ambientimage Photography has photographed the memories for about 75 couples taking the plunge for the second time around. Jacobson says the split between second-time brides and second-time grooms is about 50/50.

Jacobson says for second weddings, she sees couples planning more destination weddings with just the couple or intimate luxurious destination weddings with their closest friends and family members — about 15 to 30 guests.

From a purely photographic standpoint, second weddings and destination second weddings tend to put much more emphasis on the location, the overall vacation experience, the scenery, and planning an intimate, luxurious getaway for the couple and their honored guests. Second weddings tend to have an emphasis on the personalized details of the wedding.

Oftentimes, the little details that make every wedding personal, such as unique DIY elements, special veils, and invitations, are left out or even deemed not important during the second wedding. Perhaps the couple had this done during their first wedding and is embarrassed to do something similar for the second wedding, or their lives are busier now, and they just do not have the time to organize these details.

When the special touches are left out of the second, it also means the special touches are left out of the photographs. Adding flowers beyond just a bouquet and a boutonniere, adding personalized menus, love notes or aisle runners, even if just two people, significantly affect the mood. The difference in mood reflects in the appearance of the photographs and ensures the most beautiful setting for the photographs. By taking the time to incorporate personal details, friends and family back home can share in all the moments with couple. Some couples, in a rush to make it as simple and relaxing as possible, make it too simple. Hair and makeup are often minimized while, especially for older brides, it becomes even more important to look spectacular on your wedding day.

The intimate destination wedding allows everyone to have a carefree, relaxing, and beautiful day without any of the anxiety of planning a large-scale event, or the stress of re-inviting hundreds of guests. With much of the stress lifted, the wedding becomes an adventurous trip of a lifetime at a dream location: incredible food, elegant scenery, magical moments, and above all, making it all about the couple — and all of this shines through in the memories captured by the wedding photographer.

Interview Questions for the Photographers

During the interview with each photographer, first look at the portfolio of work. In addition, ask and find out answers to any questions you have before deciding which photographer to hire.

- What is your photography style?
- Do you shoot in digital or film?
- Will you sell me the rights?
- Will you have negatives or high-resolution images burned to a disc?
- Are you familiar with my venue(s)?

- Will you be the photographer at our wedding?
- How many hours are you available?
- Do you include any printed photographs?
- Do you make enhancements?
- Do you offer albums?
- Do you have assistants?
- Do you have backup equipment that is the same high quality?
- What are your rates?
- Do you offer packages?
- When will I be able to see the proofs?
- When will I receive my album?
- When will I receive all of my final photographs?

Photographer Comparison Chart	
Business name	
Contact person	
Address	
Telephone number	
Email address	
Fax number	

Photographer Comparison Chart	
Website	
First impression	
Portfolio impressions	
Reprint rights	
Availability	
Albums & enhancements available	
Package options	
Rates	
Payment schedule and policy	
Cancellation policy	

Picture Checklist

When you hire a photographer, work with him or her to come up with a checklist of pictures that are important to capture. Professional photographers are trained to take the photographs that capture the moments of a wedding, but it is a good idea to put in writing the moments you definitely want to emphasize. You can use the following checklist as a starting point and add any pictures in that are not already listed here.

Photographs of the bride:

- ❑ A solo portrait of the bride in her wedding gown
- ❑ A portrait of the bride with her mother
- ❑ A portrait of the bride with her father
- ❑ A portrait of the bride with her mother and her father
- ❑ A portrait of the bride with her siblings
- ❑ A portrait of the bride with her maid of honor
- ❑ A portrait of the bride with her entire bridal party
- ❑ A portrait of the bride with another special friend or family member (this could be your best friend from high school or college, your grandmother, your grandparents, or any other relationship you have that is special to you)

Photographs of the groom:

- ❑ A portrait of the groom in his tuxedo
- ❑ A portrait of the groom and his father

- ❑ A portrait of the groom and his mother
- ❑ A portrait of the groom with his father and his mother
- ❑ A portrait of the groom with his siblings
- ❑ A portrait of the groom with his best man
- ❑ A portrait of the groom with his best man and his groomsmen
- ❑ A portrait of the groom with another special friend or family member — this could be a best friend from high school or college, his grandfather, his grandparents, or any other relationship that is special to him

Other:

- ❑ Your guests arriving at the church or ceremony venue
- ❑ The ushers escorting your guests to their seats
- ❑ The guest book attendant
- ❑ The bride and her father arriving at the ceremony and getting out of the car
- ❑ The seating of the grandparents
- ❑ The seating of the groom's parents
- ❑ The seating mother of the bride
- ❑ The groom and the groomsmen standing at the altar
- ❑ Your attendants' **processional** down the aisle
- ❑ The ring bearer and flower girl
- ❑ The bride and father-of-the-bride processional
- ❑ The bride and groom exchanging their vows

- ❑ The exchanging of rings
- ❑ The first kiss of the newlyweds
- ❑ The lighting of the unity candle
- ❑ The bride and groom walking up the aisle
- ❑ The bride alone, holding her bouquet
- ❑ The bride and groom together
- ❑ The bride and groom's hands, showing their wedding rings
- ❑ Bride and groom with the bride's parents
- ❑ Bride and groom with the bride's parents and siblings
- ❑ Bride and groom with the bride's parents, siblings, and grandparents
- ❑ Bride and groom with the groom's parents
- ❑ Bride and groom with the groom's parents and siblings
- ❑ Bride and groom with the groom's parents, siblings, and grandparents
- ❑ Bride and groom with both sets of parents
- ❑ Bride and groom with both sides of the family, parents, siblings, and grandparents
- ❑ Bride and groom with the maid of honor and the best man
- ❑ Bride and groom with their wedding party
- ❑ Bride and groom getting out of the car as they arrive at the reception
- ❑ Bride and groom entering the reception
- ❑ The receiving line
- ❑ The buffet table, if you have one
- ❑ The parents' table
- ❑ The bride and groom at the head table

- ❑ The wedding party at the head table
- ❑ The toast by the best man
- ❑ The cutting of the cake
- ❑ Bride and groom feeding each other a bite of cake
- ❑ The bride and groom's first dance as husband and wife
- ❑ The bride dancing with her father
- ❑ The groom dancing with his mother
- ❑ The tossing of the wedding bouquet
- ❑ The removal and the tossing of the **garter**
- ❑ Bride and groom with the people who caught the bouquet and the garter
- ❑ The bride and groom leaving the reception

Choosing the Videographer

Now that you have ensured your smiling faces will be captured forever, you might consider a videographer to make sure the action and wishes from your friends and family are yours to enjoy for years to come. A videographer is a professional that shoots raw footage of your wedding. Typically, the videographer shoots starting with the bride

and groom getting ready for the ceremony, and continues to record footage through the end of the reception. The majority of a videographer's work starts after the wedding is over. The videographer is responsible for editing and preparing the raw footage of the wedding to turn it into a wedding DVD with special effects, background music, and other graphics that you discuss with the videographer ahead of time.

There are a couple things you should look for when choosing a videographer. First, you will want to see some clips from his or her previous shoots. Is the camera held steady? Is it a good angle so that you can see the important parts of the scenes? Are there miscellaneous things entering into the camera frame that should not be there, such as tree limbs, candles, or people walking in front of the vows? However, do not base your decision solely on the video. Ask the photographer his or her philosophy on how obtrusive to be when recording your wedding. A beautiful film of you and your fiancé sweetly reciting your vows is one thing. Being distracted during the vows by a camera two inches from your nose or tripping over a tripod leg on your way up the aisle is a scene you do not want on your big day.

Because it is so hard to base your decision on the final result alone, ask any of your recently married friends for recommendations to see if anyone had a videographer they absolutely loved. Alternately, try reading testimonials or reviews online to see if any company or videographer has a glowing reputation among the online wedding community. If you have hired a wedding planner, he or she should have some recommendations from his or her contacts within the industry.

As you meet with different videographers, use this chart to record the information. Later, when you sit down to decide which videographer offers the services and packages that best fit your needs, you can use these charts to perform a side-by-side comparison.

Videographer Comparison Chart	
Business name	
Contact person	
Address	
Telephone number	
Email address	
Fax number	
Website	
First impression	
Portfolio impressions	
Availability	
Enhancements and editing	
Package options	
Rates	

Videographer Comparison Chart	
Payment schedule and policy	
Cancellation policy	

Interview Questions for the Videographers

As with the photographers, you will want to sit down with your videographer to get an idea of the quality of his or her work, the reliability of his or her videography team, and the personality you will be dealing before, during, and after the wedding. Here is a list of questions to ask potential videographers:

- Do you have samples of your work?
- Do you shoot in high definition?
- Are you familiar with my venues?
- Do you have assistants?
- Will you be the one taking the video at my wedding?
- Do you offer editing as part of your rates?
- Do you have backup equipment?
- What are your rates?
- Do you offer packages?
- How much will it cost to get extra copies of the video?
- When will I receive my completed wedding video?

Video Checklist

When you hire a videographer, work with him or her to come up with a checklist of scenes that are important to capture. Professional videographers will know how to watch for the most memorable moments at a wedding and will tape them as unobtrusively as possible, but it is a good idea to put in writing the moments you definitely want to emphasize. You can use the following checklist as a starting point and add any scenes in that are not already listed here.

- ❏ Clips of the bride getting ready
- ❏ Shots of the bridal party and mother helping the bride get ready
- ❏ Footage of the bride's father coming to get her to escort her down the aisle
- ❏ Clips of the groom getting ready
- ❏ Shots of the groomsmen helping the groom get ready
- ❏ Your guests arriving at the church or ceremony venue
- ❏ The ushers escorting your guests to their seats
- ❏ The bride and her father arriving at the ceremony and getting out of the car
- ❏ The seating of the grandparents
- ❏ The seating of the groom's parents
- ❏ The seating of the mother of the bride
- ❏ The groom and the groomsmen standing at the altar
- ❏ Your attendants' processional down the aisle
- ❏ The ring bearer and flower girl
- ❏ The bride and father-of-the-bride processional

- ❑ The bride and groom exchanging their vows
- ❑ The exchanging of rings
- ❑ The first kiss of the newlyweds
- ❑ The lighting of the unity candle
- ❑ The bride and groom walking up the aisle
- ❑ The bride and groom's hands, showing their wedding rings
- ❑ Bride and groom with their wedding party
- ❑ Bride and groom getting out of the car as they arrive at the reception
- ❑ Bride and groom entering the reception
- ❑ The receiving line
- ❑ The buffet table, if you have one
- ❑ The parents' table
- ❑ The bride and groom at the head table
- ❑ The wedding party at the head table
- ❑ The toast by the best man
- ❑ The cutting of the cake
- ❑ Bride and groom feeding each other a bite of cake
- ❑ The bride and groom's first dance as husband and wife
- ❑ The bride dancing with her father
- ❑ The groom dancing with his mother
- ❑ The tossing of the wedding bouquet
- ❑ The removal and the tossing of the garter
- ❑ Bride and groom with the people who caught the bouquet and garter
- ❑ The bride and groom leaving the reception

Money-Saving Tips

Money-saving tip #1: Contact the art department of your local college, universities, or schools. Photography students typically freelance to shoot weddings for a small fee, class credit, or the experience. When you work with a student photographer, they will shoot the wedding, and then you are responsible for printing the pictures and putting together your own wedding albums. You should view their portfolios and ask the same questions you would when hiring a "professional" wedding photographer.

Money-saving tip #2: Find amateur or new photographers on websites, such as Craigslist (**www.craigslist.org**), eBay® Classifieds (**www.ebayclassifieds.com**), and Backpage (**www.backpage.com**). Search for freelance photographers looking for work, or post your own free ad searching for a wedding photographer. Because amateur and new photographers are looking for experience to break into the wedding industry, it might cost you $200 to $500 to pay them to shoot your wedding. You should view their portfolios and ask the same questions you would when hiring a "professional" wedding photographer.

Money-saving tip #3: Obtain the negatives or photos you can copy on a CD-ROM. Negotiate ownership of these items, so you do not have to pay the photographer every time you want to print a picture or print multiple pictures to put together your own wedding album.

Money-saving tip #4: Hire a photographer that charges a fee for his or her time and for the number of pictures taken. You can limit the number of hours and pictures to cut back on your photography bill.

Money-saving tip #5: Opt out of the videographer. A wedding video is great, but it can be an added expense. Married couples agree that they might pull out the video on their one-year anniversary, if that. Ask yourself if paying thousands of dollars for a video is worth it when you might watch the video once or twice for the rest of your life.

Money-saving tip #6: Hire a professional videographer to shoot raw footage of the wedding, and ask for an unedited video. The majority of the cost you pay to a videographer is for the time it takes to edit the video. Choose to keep the raw footage as your keepsake or hire a freelance editor to turn the raw footage into the wedding video you want.

Money-saving tip #7: If you have an aspiring filmmaker or videographer in your family, ask them to shoot the wedding video for you. They are the ones that typically have a video camera in their hands anyway, so they probably will not mind. Ask for a copy of the raw footage. Either keep it as is or pay to have a professional edit it.

With your wedding memories captured in time, you and your guests have the opportunity to relive your wedding day time and time again. Now that you know the options you have for capturing the moments of your wedding, it is time to talk about what might just be the sweetest aspect of the wedding reception — the cake. *Chapter 13 covers the details on finding a bakery to create the confection of your dreams.*

CHAPTER THIRTEEN

Let Them Eat Cake

One of the tastiest parts of planning your second wedding is picking out the wedding cake. With several different wedding cake options, it can be a dizzying process, but it does not have to be. In this chapter, you will discover several options for choosing the traditional wedding cake and the other types of desserts available for weddings, such as the **groom's cake**. The chapter also reveals alternatives to traditional cakes and ways to have the cake you want but save money at the same time. So, as Marie Antoinette would say, "Let them eat cake!"

Wedding Cake

Choosing the wedding cake you want starts from the outside and works its way to the inside. Not only does choosing a cake consist of the way it looks, but it is also about the way it tastes. You can choose from an

almost unlimited number of looks, such as a cake with one, two, three, or more tiers. You might even have your cake designer bake the wedding cake into a particular design, such as a hatbox, or another design you rip from the pages of a bridal magazine.

The way the wedding cake looks on the outside has a lot to do with the type of frosting or icing you choose. The three icing types include:

- **Fondant icing** is smooth and neat and does not look like icing at all. If you are looking for a design with a smooth and defined look, then fondant icing is the way to go. Unfortunately, fondant is also expensive, does not have as much taste as other types of icing, and can be difficult to cut.

- **Butter Cream icing** has a sweeter taste and allows for almost any decorating you want. This type of icing is less expensive than fondant and can provide a similar smooth look of fondant.

- **Whipped Cream icing** has a lighter and less rich taste than butter cream icing. This type of icing is the least expensive of the three finishing options. Whipped cream icing melts in heat or humid climates, and it does not lend itself well to many types of decorations.

Once you choose the shape, style, and topping for the wedding cake, it is time to choose the flavor. When it comes to wedding cakes, the sky is the limit on the number of options you have. Not only do you have the option to choose the flavor of the cake, but you also have the option to add a filling.

Some of the cake flavors available include:

- White
- Yellow
- Chocolate
- Carrot
- Spice
- Chocolate
- Mocha
- Lemon chiffon
- Orange chiffon
- Raspberry truffle
- Chocolate mousse
- Almond
- Hazelnut
- Red velvet
- Marble

Some of the fillings available include the following:

- Hazelnut
- Raspberry
- Mocha

- Pineapple
- Cream cheese
- Strawberry mousse or crème
- Chocolate mousse or crème
- Amaretto custard or crème
- Lemon mousse or crème

But remember. The sky is the limit when choosing flavors and fillings. If you do not see what you want at one bakery, visit another or ask for a custom flavoring.

Groom's Cake

The groom's cake has been a tradition in southern culture for years. It is also a tradition showing up at more and more wedding receptions. Traditionally, the groom's cake slices are put in boxes and sent home with the unmarried girls at the wedding to place it under their pillow and dream about their future groom.

Today, the groom's cake is meant to be a reflection of the groom himself — his hobbies, likes, favorite sports, profession, alma mater, or anything else of significant value to him. Therefore, the groom's cake can be fun, but if you are trying to save money, it is easy to do so here. Here are some tips:

- Make the groom's cake yourself or, for more fun, have the best man and the groom's attendants make the cake. They likely will have a great time doing it.
- Ask for a discount with your baker. Many bakeries offer the groom's cake at a reduced fee.
- Skip the groom's cake altogether if it is not important to your fiancé.

Choosing the Bakery

Now that you know your likes and dislikes, it is time to choose your bakery. You have three primary sources to consider when choosing your wedding cake:

1. **Commercial bakeries**, such as grocery stores. The prices are reasonable, but personalization options are few. Commercial bakeries do not always offer as many choices for wedding cakes, as part of the savings comes with choosing a standard wedding cake.

2. **Caterers and/or reception sites** might offer a wedding-cake service. At times, you can find a great deal if you go this route because it is part of the package. Other times, these types of services cost significantly more than you can find on your own. The same goes with quality. Sometimes it is terrific; other times it is not.

3. **Small bakers and/or pastry chefs** are where you will find the most creative, spectacular cakes. Although they can be difficult to find and are often of significant cost, the quality and appearance of your wedding cake will be superb. When you begin searching for the bakery that will make your cake, here are a few ideas you might have overlooked, as well as some sources:

- If your family has a regular bakery for birthday cakes, anniversaries, and other special moments, it could be your best bet. You already know it is reliable, you know if its cakes are a quality product, and even better, you might have a relationship with it already. This relationship could garner you a discount.

- If a friend was recently married and you admired her wedding cake, ask her who created it. Some bakers offer a discount based on referrals, so be sure to mention you were referred when contacting them.

- Other wedding industry professionals. Florists and photographers attend many weddings, so they know which bakers are the best in the business. Ask for their recommendations based on your needs.

- Ask the manager of your reception venue for a referral. He or she sees wedding after wedding and has certainly noticed what cakes stood out and which did not.

- Watch the advertisements in your newspaper for people who make wedding cakes from their home or as a side job. Be sure to ask for references and to see pictures if you go this route.

- Bridal shows are an excellent location to learn more about bakeries in your area. They also tend to have samples of their cakes to taste.

When you go on your appointments to meet with bakers, take copies of these comparison sheets along with you. The charts allow you to keep notes during your meetings that you can review later. It will help you keep the information straight because it quickly can become confusing when you meet with multiple bakers.

Baker Comparison Chart	
Company name	
Contact person	
Address	
Telephone number	
Email address	
Fax number	
Website	
First impression	
Impressions at tasting	
Cake flavor choices	
Will they coordinate with the florist?	
Availability	
Rates	
Special packages available	
Do they offer delivery and setup?	

Baker Comparison Chart	
Is there a delivery fee?	
Payment schedule and policy	
Cancellation policy	

Interview Questions for the Bakery

As you begin looking around for the bakery to create your wedding cake, ask these questions:

- Will the cake designer create a custom cake, based on your specifications? If not, are there styles you can view to choose? This is a good time to show any pictures you have clipped out.

- What are the most popular cake designs and flavors?

- Ask what types of ingredients the baker uses. Remember, the fresher the ingredients, the better quality cake you will have.

- Can you sample any cakes? You will have an easier time deciding on flavors and fillings if you can taste test them.

- How many people are involved in the creation of your cake? Some bakeries use only one person per cake, while others have bakers and designers.

- When is the cake prepared in relation to your wedding? The less time the cake sits in the freezer, the higher quality it will be.

- If you decide to use fresh flowers to decorate the cake, does the baker work with your florist, or does it have another it does business with? This could affect your price, as you are more likely to receive a discount from the florist who is handling all your wedding day blooms.

- How many wedding cakes are being prepared for the same day as your wedding?

- Find out how the baker prices its cakes. Is it by the slice, which is the industry standard, or is it by the cake? Ask to see a price list that details the costs for flavors, fillings, and icings.

- Are there any extra charges to be aware of?

- Many bakeries will throw in the top tier of the cake free (this is the tier that couples save for their first anniversary). Ask if the bakeries you are considering offer this.

- Ask if the baker is licensed by the state health department. If it is not, you will want to look elsewhere.

- Does the bakery, or cake designer, deliver the finished wedding cake to the reception? If it does not, realize that you will have to arrange delivery, and wedding cakes in transit are an accident waiting to happen. If the bakery offers delivery services, is there a charge for this service, and what is the fee?

- Will the bakery pick up the cake board and pillars, if used, after the reception, or do you need to return them?

Money-Saving Tips

Money-saving tip #1: In most cases, you will get a lower price from a baker than a caterer.

Money-saving tip #2: Consider layers instead of tiers. Tiers cost more money.

Money-saving tip #3: Avoid handmade sugar flowers and molded shapes to cut costs.

Money-saving tip #4: When choosing your cake style, decorations, and intricacies, realize that just like everything else, time is money. The longer it takes to make your cake, the more expensive it will be.

Money-saving tip #5: Call a local craft store that offers cake-decorating classes, and ask if the teacher bakes and designs wedding cakes on a freelance basis.

Money-saving tip #6: Do not overlook the "superstores." Walmart®, Sam's Club®, BJ's®, or Costco® offer a tremendous deal on wedding cakes. They will let you sample them as well.

Money-saving tip #7: Make your own wedding cake or have someone close to you make it. You do not have to have a glamorous cake — just one that is attractive and tastes great. Check with Wilton (**www.wilton.com**) for ideas.

Money-saving tip #8: Find a baker that will create a cake that is part real and part fake. This works best with cakes that have multiple tiers. The bottom tier is real, so you can use it for the cake cutting ceremony. Buy sheet cakes for cutting in the kitchen and serve these to your guests instead of serving slices from a "real" wedding cake. Sheet cakes do not have to have decorations and shave a great deal of the cost out of the budget for your wedding cake.

Money-saving tip #9: Skip the wedding cake altogether and offer alternative desserts or a dessert bar instead. You can have a cake or dessert buffet, where guests can choose their own dessert options. You might even consider a candy bar, where you fill dishes up with candies that match your wedding colors. Add scoopers and favor boxes or bags, so guests can scoop the candies they want to eat at the reception or when they arrive home.

With the sweetest part of the wedding out of the way, it is time to move on to deciding what to wear. *Chapter 14 covers the attire and accessories for all of the important roles in the wedding — from the bride and groom to the attendants, flower girl, and ring bearer.*

CHAPTER FOURTEEN

What to Wear

Your wedding day is your big day, and you want to look the part. It is your starring role. From the dress and shoes to the jewelry and veil, you want to shimmer and shine. Not only do you want to look great as you make your debut on the aisle, but you also want to feel great, too. In this chapter, you will uncover the attire for everyone in the wedding party, from you and the groom to your bridal party and wedding guests. Accessories, such as jewelry, veils, hair decorations, and shoes are also part of the deal. The chapter also provides information on how to inform your guests what they should wear so that it coordinates with the style of the wedding. The end of the chapter also includes some money-saving tips when shopping for various types of wedding attire and accessories.

Bride's Attire

The wedding gown is really the focal point of the bride's attire for the day of the wedding. Start by choosing the wedding gown. Once you have the gown or dress you are going to wear, you have the foundational piece on which to build on in choosing the veil, jewelry, shoes, and other accessories.

This is especially true because these other accessories should match and coordinate with the style of the gown.

The wedding gown

You might have heard many brides say they "just knew" when they tried on that perfect wedding gown. Some brides, however, need a little more time to find the gown of their dreams.

The best place to start looking for your gown is in bridal magazines. This is an efficient and inexpensive way to see the current styles available. While looking at the magazines, rip out the pages of the gowns you like and bring them with you to the bridal shop. The retailers will be able to help you find the ones you want quickly and help you try them on.

The style of your wedding dress should match the style or formality of your wedding. If you are planning a large, expensive, black-tie wedding, then you should wear a princess-style ball gown; however, even if you are getting married in the backyard and serving barbecue, you are entitled to wear a formal gown — it is your wedding day.

Begin looking for your bridal gown at least nine months before your wedding. This is because it can take up to six months to receive the dress, and you might need to have it altered to fit you perfectly.

Think about the details you know you are looking for in your wedding gown. Use the following table to determine which wedding gown style is right for you:

- **Material:** Silk, satin, lace, taffeta, **tulle**, velvet, charmeuse, crepe, damask, chiffon, brocade, jersey, **organza**, dupioni
- **Length:** Cocktail, ankle-length, full-length
- **Neckline:** Sweetheart, halter, strapless, square, scoop, V-neck, portrait, bateau, off-the-shoulder
- **Sleeves:** Sleeveless, cap, ¾-length, full, bell, puffed, fitted
- **Silhouette:** A-line, fitted, sheath, ball-gown, dropped, empire, mermaid
- **Train:** None, sweeping, chapel, semi-cathedral, cathedral, royal
- **Color:** White, cream, champagne, rose, or any other color imaginable

To see many of the above-mentioned options for yourself, visit **www.preownedweddingdresses.com/general-information/ wedding-dress-101.html** for diagrams and more wedding dress options.

On this last point, whether or not a second bride should wear white, is probably where you will run into the most debate in your own mind and from the opinions of your family and friends. Traditionally, a white wedding gown stands for the purity of the bride, meaning that she is a virgin when she marries her husband. A second bride, especially one with children, does not fit into this traditional mold. Although many frown upon a second bride wearing white, in the end, you should choose the style AND color that looks the best on you. Just realize that there may be some whispers as you make your debut down the aisle.

If You Are:	What is the Best Gown for You?	Avoid
Slender/ short	Simple styles are best. A straight or slight A-line dress will add height. A gown with princess seams that is not too full will also make you look taller.	Dresses with heavy beadwork or beaded lace, as this will camouflage the princess seams, having the opposite effect. Also, stay away from overly full or puffed sleeves, which will make you appear wider and shorter. Gathered or tiered skirts will also appear to minimize your height.
Full-figured/ short	Seek out styles that will make your figure appear longer and leaner. Vertical silhouette lines, such as the A-line, princess, and straight styles will help achieve this. Look for gowns that skim your body and flow without hugging your curves too much.	Heavy, shiny fabrics tend to make the body look heavier. Bouffant or tiered silhouettes and an overly full veil should be avoided, as they will give the illusion of added bulk. Stay away from larger prints, even in the same color.
Average/ average	You have many more options available to you, but consider gowns with defined waistlines and gathered skirts. The sheath and fitted gowns are good choices.	Nothing to steer clear from. Try on a few styles and see which flatter your exact body shape the best.

If You Are:	What is the Best Gown for You?	Avoid
Full-figured/average	Styles that will be the most slenderizing for this body type are the A-line, princess, and empire gowns. Keep an eye out for dresses that flow easily over the hips and do not gather tightly around the waist. Any of the lighter, thin, and soft fabrics will be the most attractive.	Stay away from very large and very small prints. Also, heavier fabrics, as well as heavily beaded gowns, should be avoided. Round necklines may not be the most appealing, depending on the shape of your face.
Slender/tall	Almost any of the standard styles will be appealing on this body type. If you are very slender, you may want to consider dresses that extend past the silhouette. Tiered skirts, French bustles, and beaded laces will add fullness to a slender figure.	For brides who do not want to appear taller than they already are, sheath-style gowns should be avoided, as well as any other straight-falling dress. Another consideration — shorter veils, such as the blush veil, may appear too short as compared to the height of a tall bride.
Full-figured/tall	The full-figured tall bride will want to look for slenderizing styles of gowns. The A-line, princess, and empire gowns are all excellent choices, as they will accentuate the height of the bride, and help them appear slimmer.	Heavier fabrics, heavy beading, full skirts, puffed sleeves, and gathered waists will likely not be the best choices. Anything that adds bulk or clutter will make the full-figured bride appear larger than she is.

Because choosing a dress is such a crucial part of the wedding-planning process, many brides bring people with them when they try on wedding gowns. It is up to you whom you decide to bring, but most brides make this a bonding experience with their mother, stepmother, mother-in-law, maid of honor, other bridal party members, siblings, close friends, or any mix of these people. It is important to have someone you trust to give an honest opinion. These people will be able to share in your happiness — and your potential anxiety.

When you head out to the bridal boutiques, follow these tips to make the process easier:

- Wear appropriate underwear, similar to what you might wear under your gown on your wedding day. For example, if you know you want a strapless dress, make sure you have a strapless bra, or bustier-style strapless bra.

- Pull your hair up to keep it out of your way and keep you cool while trying on big dresses.

- Bring a bottle of water — you likely will get hot trying on so many gowns.

- Bring a support group to give you honest opinions.

- Bring sample pictures of gowns you like.

- Wear shoes with the same height of heel you plan to wear on your wedding day. If you have not chosen your shoes yet, bring a couple of different pairs with different heights of the heel so you can see how the style of the shoe looks with the dress.

- Have someone photograph you from different angles in gowns you try on.

When looking for that perfect wedding gown, it is important to keep an open mind. A dress that you might not consider at first glance might be stunning once you put it on. You might want to try several bridal boutiques to ensure you find the dress of your dreams. In the past, many bridal boutiques had their own seamstresses. This made it easy to take measurements and have alterations done within the same company. These days, fewer bridal boutiques employ seamstresses, so it might be necessary to find a local shop or an independent contractor for alterations.

Alternative wedding gowns and bridal attire

White and wedding often come to mind when it comes to a wedding dress. Especially for a second wedding, white, or even ivory, is not the only color a bride can wear while walking down the aisle. Second brides have the option to wear a wedding dress or wedding suit in any color they want to wear.

A few of the colors to consider include:

- Red/garnet/crimson (common tradition in Asian weddings for good luck and can bring good luck to an American wedding, too)
- Blue (It can be the something blue and something new for the wedding traditions.)
- Yellow (great for a spring theme or springtime wedding)
- Violet/purple/lilac (also a nice color for a spring wedding)
- Pink/blush (bring new meaning to the blushing bride with a dress or suit in the color pink or blush)

With second weddings more common than not, you can find dresses and suits in alternative colors at traditional bridal shops. You also can find wedding suits and formal dresses in colors other than white and ivory at department stores, dress boutiques, second-hand stores, consignment shops, and more.

Keep in mind brides do not have to wear a formal gown officially named as a wedding dress either. It is just as proper to choose a formal gown that is not a wedding dress. Again, you can buy formal gowns at dress boutiques, department stores, bridal shops, and many other types of clothing stores.

Bride's Accessories

When it comes to dressing the bride, it is about more than just the dress. It is about the whole package, which includes the bride's garter, shoes, jewelry, and other accessories. Depending on the style of the wedding and the style of the bride's dress or suit, not all of the accessories will apply. For example, a second-time bride that is wearing a wedding suit might choose not to don a veil. A bride and groom that are not tossing the garter at the reception would not need to buy a garter for the bride to wear.

Garter

Many brides wear a garter for the tradition of having grooms remove the garter from their legs during the reception for the garter-tossing portion of the reception. Just as the bride throws her bouquet to the eligible women guests, the groom throws the garter to the eligible men. The bride will sit in a chair in the center of the reception as the groom reaches under her gown to retrieve the garter. He will then throw it to the eligible bachelors. It is the belief that whoever catches  the garter will be the next man to marry. At some weddings, the man who catches the garter will place it on the leg of the woman who caught the bouquet. Also, brides use their garter to incorporate "something blue" into their attire.

If the bride and groom both have been married before or are not having a traditional wedding, tossing the garter is a tradition that typically is left out in a second wedding. However, if the garter toss is part of the reception, the bride and groom can incorporate hobbies or a style for the garter that matches the bride's attire. For example, brides and grooms might choose to honor their alma maters with a garter made of material with the college mascot. Brides wearing a crimson wedding gown might opt for a matching crimson garter or a color that complements the dress color.

Shoes

Bridal boutiques carry a selection of shoes and often can dye them to match your wedding gown. Ultimately, there is no limit to the shoe stores you can visit to find the perfect pair. Remember that you will be on your feet for a long time, so you may want to consider comfort as well as fashion. Some brides choose to change shoes after the traditional portion of the ceremony. Although you could choose to wear stilettos with your gown, you might also choose to change into a pair of flats for the reception. Some brides even purchase white sneakers and decorate them with things like lace and ribbons. Depending on your dress, your feet might be completely covered, so others cannot even see your shoes.

Remember that heels are not the only shoes that hurt your feet. Ballet slippers and flip flops have a lack of support, which means you will feel like you are walking directly on a hard surfaces. They can be just as painful as wearing a high heel.

Jewelry for the bride

The jewelry you choose to wear is completely personal and will need to be chosen based on your gown. Some brides wear diamonds; others wear pearls. Some select other gemstones, while others opt to wear nothing but their engagement and wedding ring.

Traditionally, brides often choose jewelry that is a family heirloom, such as wearing grandma's pearls that all of the women in the family have worn during their walk down the aisle. If you are not a second-time bride, then wearing the family heirloom carries on the tradition. If you are walking down the aisle for the second time, you might choose to wear the same pearls you wore in your first wedding, or you might wish to choose a different piece of jewelry from the family jewels.

Here is a tip for your wedding ceremony: Wear your engagement ring on your right hand. This way, the groom will be able to slip your wedding ring onto your left hand. You wear your wedding ring closest to your heart, with your engagement ring stacked on top of that. After the ceremony, you can slip your engagement ring back onto your left hand.

Jewelry for the kids

If one or both of you have children, you also should consider exchanging symbols of the new bond with them. A nice touch might be to give the children a charm necklace, bracelet, or ring that represents your commitment to them in the joining of your two families into one new family. As an added bonus, you even can consider buying yourselves a matching set of jewelry so that you all have matching pieces — the children, the bride, and the groom.

Veil

You can wear anything from a short, fingertip veil to a cathedral-length veil, or even no veil at all. The best place to purchase your veil is at the bridal boutique. If they do not have the veil you want, ask if they can order it. If they cannot, consult with your tailor to see if something can be made.

When choosing your veil, consider how you will wear your hair and whether you will be wearing a special headpiece. This is important because it will dictate how your veil attaches to your hair. Make sure you bring your veil with you to the hair salon for your trial hairstyles — the way the veil fits will make a difference.

Some second-time brides choose to skip the veil altogether. This is especially true if the bride is not wearing a traditional wedding gown but has chosen a wedding gown alternative. Veil styles tend to match the style of the bride's attire. For example, if the bride is wearing a red wedding suit, she could choose a matching red hat. For brides who wish to wear a suit and a veil, a short veil is more appropriate than the floor-length veil that matches a formal wedding gown.

Headpiece

A headpiece is more than just a veil. Most brides wear their headpieces through the entire reception, even after taking off their veil. Some brides choose to wear a headpiece in place of a veil and, again, wear it throughout the ceremony and the reception. The headpiece you choose may be based on how you want to wear your hair, or you might fall in love with a headpiece and choose your hairstyle accordingly.

It is popular for brides to choose a **tiara** as their headpiece — after all, a woman does not get to wear a tiara that often. A wedding gown and a tiara can make a woman feel like a princess on her wedding day. A tiara is also versatile when it comes to hairstyles and veils. Other headpiece options include combs, barrettes, pins, ponytail holders, bun holders, and headbands. All of these can be incorporated into the hairstyle and can look beautiful and elegant.

CASE STUDY: DRESS FOR THE OCCASION

Bridal Couture Girls
Leslie Freude-Holtzclaw
26916 Via Terraza
Santa Clarita, CA 91350
661-373-9088
leslie@bridalcouturegirls.com
www.bridalcouturegirls.com

Getting married the second time can be a much different experience than the first time, especially for the bride. Most brides know what they want when it comes to their wedding attire. The attire details are an expression of the bride and groom's life together.

Wedding attire changes with the trends. Second weddings reflect the bride's stage of life, so if she is into vintage-style attire, then the second wedding is the chance to make this style her own.

The bride style reflects this newfound happiness, and the accessory pieces are statement pieces. The wedding dress is simpler version of the first wedding dress, so it is typically chiffon, satin in blush, ivory, or champagne. A bride may add pearls and a sash to complete the look.

Brides tend to select birdcage veils, which reflect a more mature elegance, while the first-time bride wears a blusher veil as a tradition. Some wear something decorative in their hair, though not necessarily a veil. Second, Bridal Couture Girls also see bridal accessories handed down or the bride turns family heirlooms into a special accessory. Bridal Couture Girls can take any family heirloom and make it a fabulous statement piece for the bride, from a broach to bringing in part of the mother or grandmother's gown.

The attire reflects who the bride and groom are, and most second weddings stray away from the traditional wedding attire. Second brides are wearing cocktail length dresses and couture suits they can wear again. The attire for the groom and the wedding party does not change as much in the second wedding from the first wedding. Again, there attire reflects the theme of the wedding. Bridal Couture Girls are seeing more grooms wearing everyday suits instead of tuxedos.

Bridesmaid's Attire

Now, it is time to dress the women you have chosen for your bridal party. Most brides ask for their bridesmaids' input when choosing the bridal party attire.

The dresses

The **maid of honor** and bridesmaids are traditionally responsible for paying for their own dresses and alterations. Consider your dress options carefully, and make your decision based on what looks best on each of the bridesmaids you have because their figures, shapes, and sizes will most likely vary.

You have the option of having your maid of honor's dress look slightly different from the other bridesmaids, so she stands out in her important role. Other brides choose a uniform look for all of the women in the bridal party, regardless of their role. One look for all of the women in the bridal party, regardless of their role. One option for bridal parties of different shapes, sizes, and figures is to choose separates — a skirt and top — that can be paired together. This allows each bridesmaid to pick the top and bottom that looks best on her, but keeps the color scheme you want.

Finally, you may allow the women in your bridal party to choose their own dress based on your color scheme. This allows the bridesmaids to pick a dress that fits them and even allows them to wear the dress on more than one occasion after your wedding.

Bridesmaid's Accessories

Putting together the right look for the bridesmaids goes beyond the dress, suit, or other clothing they wear. Adding accessories, such as shoes and jewelry, help to complete the overall appearance of the wedding party.

Shoes

The bridal party members are going to be on their feet just as much as you on your wedding day as they run around to get things done. It is important to consider this when choosing their shoes. If you want a uniform look, then choose the same shoes for each person, and simply have them send their sizes and payments. But you might want to offer your bridal party the option of choosing their own shoes. You can set limits, such as no flats, no open-toe, and no wedges. You also can dictate the color. If you want the shoes dyed to match the dresses, then they will need to purchase **dyeable** shoes. The shoes all should be dyed at the same time to ensure they are all exactly the same color.

Jewelry

You might choose to take care of jewelry options by giving them jewelry as their thank-you gift at the rehearsal dinner; otherwise, do not expect them to go out and buy diamond earrings because that is what you want them to wear. You can make demands, but keep them reasonable.

You might tell your bridal party that you prefer them to wear only silver or gold jewelry. You could ask them not to wear necklaces, bracelets, anklets, or rings, the exception being their own wedding and engagement rings. You might also tell them not to wear hoop or dangling earrings.

Jewelry can be expensive, so do not have high expectations unless you will provide it.

Groom's Attire

The groom also is going to garner much attention on the wedding day, and he should be dressed in an outfit that complements the bride. The formality of the outfit the groom chooses likely will be based on the formality of the wedding, as well as what the bride will be wearing. It is not common knowledge that these suits and tuxedos are further categorized, so you can choose the appropriate attire for your wedding:

- **Morning suit:** A morning suit is for formal, morning weddings. Traditionally, it has a single button at the waist and a single tail in the back. It should be either black or grey and is worn with striped suit trousers.

- **Tuxedo or black tie:** Most often black or grey, there are many styles to choose from, with different buttons and lapels. By tradition, these are worn only in the evening but can be acceptable at any time of the day.

- **Tails:** Tails are quite formal and are worn with suspenders and a bow tie.

- **Dinner jacket:** The dinner jacket may be worn with formal trousers. It is more casual and can be worn in white or cream. Typically, it is worn with a necktie. It is acceptable in the afternoon or evening and is appropriate for summer weddings, destination weddings, or other warm-climate weddings.

- **Suit:** The standard suit is the attire of choice for a casual wedding.

You can check out some illustrations of the groom's attire choices at **www.dummies.com/how-to/content/choosing-a-tuxedo-or-suit-for-your-wedding-day.html**.

Neckwear

The first accessory item to consider is the neckwear. There are three typical options: a necktie, **bow tie**, or **ascot**. Each of these has significance when it comes to the formality of the wedding and the time of day. It is rare to see a groom wearing an ascot, which is a narrow neckband with wide, pointed wings, but it traditionally is suggested when wearing a morning suit. However, a necktie also is considered acceptable. Bow ties were the most common neckwear worn with tuxedos. Though they are still popular, neckties worn with vests

have become the more common trend. The neckwear the groom chooses also might be dictated by whether the groom wears a vest or a **cummerbund**. If wearing a cummerbund, a bow tie is the best option. If the groom chooses to wear a vest, he may select whichever feels or looks better.

The groom should opt for a vest or cummerbund and neckwear to match the bride's outfit. This is also true when it comes to a **pocket square**, which is a small piece of fabric similar to a handkerchief, worn in the outer-left breast pocket of the jacket. Also, consider the colors of the wedding, including what the women in the bridal party will wear. Bring swatches to the shop when choosing the wedding-day attire.

Tuxedo	
Types	**Comments on Style**
Double-breasted	A double-breasted jacket can effectively camouflage a larger-sized groom or groomsman. Things to look for: Make sure the size is correct, and try on several different cuts/styles to find the right one.
Cutaway	This is the traditional morning coat. The swallowtail lines on the cutaway will be attractive on almost any frame. This is an excellent choice if the groomsmen are of varied heights and body shapes.
High vest	This style works best on men who are not broad in their upper torso. For men who are broad in this area but really want this style, the vest should be in a muted shade for the best look. If your groom is on the slender side, he can do anything he wants with patterns and colors.
Low vest	Low vests are attractive on almost all body types. Just as with the high vest, broad men should go for muted shades, while smaller men can be freer with patterns and colors.
Mandarin/banded collar	For men with a thicker, shorter neck, this collar will not work well. A lay-down collar would be a better choice.
Peaked lapel	The peaked tuxedo lapel is a great choice for shorter men, as it will make the body appear longer because it draws the eye up and out, creating length. This is also a good choice for taller men.
Shawl collar	Shawl collars come in a variety of widths, and this makes them difficult to adhere to a certain body shape. Pay attention to the width and to the lines of the tux itself, and just try your eye.

Tuxedo	
Types	Comments on Style
Single-breasted (one- or two-button)	This is the most classic of all tux jackets and will look terrific on most body shapes. Taller men should go for a two-button jacket, while shorter men should go for the one-button. The more shirt that shows means it creates a longer visual line, so shorter men should use that style to add the appearance of height.
Single-breasted (three- or four-button)	This is an ultra-popular jacket. These high-buttoning jackets are amazing on tall, slender men. Heavier men should consider the one or two button version.
Tails	This is about as formal as a tuxedo gets. Unfortunately, this style sometimes can be unflattering on short or heavy men. It really depends on the length of their legs, as even short men can look great in tails.

Shoes

In most cases, grooms and groomsmen wear black shoes and socks with their wedding day attire unless they are wearing a light-colored suit or jacket. Just like the bride, the groom is on his feet for most of the wedding day. This means shoes should be comfortable as well as stylish. Wear the wedding-day shoes around the house to break them in.

Groomsmen Attire

Although some grooms choose the attire for all the men in the bridal party, you might want to consult the best man, or any of the other men, when choosing which suit or tuxedo they will wear the day of the wedding.

The men in the bridal party should all wear suits similar to the groom's suit or tuxedo. This does not mean the suits need to be the same, but they should at least be similar in style and color. However, they should be set apart slightly from the groom. This is true for the best man, as well, and this can be done in several ways.

The easiest way to set the groom apart from the best man and the groomsmen is to wear different-colored vests or cummerbunds and neckwear. When it comes to the best man and groomsmen, many couples choose accessories that will match the bridesmaids' dresses. Another way to set everyone apart is with boutonnieres, or with different fabric squares.

Shoes

Some couples want their bridal party to look uniform, and this can include shoes. Not all black dress shoes look alike, and it can make a big difference in photographs. Suit rental shops also rent shoes. This is the easiest way for you to coordinate shoes for all the men in the bridal party. However, if you do not care about exact matching, allow the men in your bridal party to rent or buy their own shoes — just specify the color.

Other Wedding Party Attire

With the bride, groom, and bridal party out of the way, it is time to decide on the look for the little people in the wedding — the kids. The parents also play a role in the bridal party, so what they wear as they make their debut down the aisle is an important factor to consider, too.

The flower girl

As the bride, you get to choose this dress for your flower girl. Some brides choose the flower-girl dress based on their own gown; some even go so far as to have a smaller version of their own gown made for the flower girl. The style and color of the dress should match the rest of the bridal party.

You might have a little more difficulty finding shoes that will mesh well with those you plan to wear or that the rest of your bridal party will wear because you do not want to put kids in heels. Although traditional shops sell children's shoes for weddings, the styles are usually child-appropriate, so you will have to match the shoes with what the kids are wearing. You will want your flower girl to be comfortable, and in any case, those shoes likely will be taken off long before the reception is over. If you want the shoes dyed to match those of the rest of the bridal party, make sure they are put with the rest of the order. Again, this will ensure that they are all the same color.

The parents

Along with the bride, groom, and bridal party, both sets of parents are going to be in the spotlight. This means they might want to dress up as well. If the parents decide to follow the standard guidelines, they should consider these attire possibilities.

The mother of the bride and the mother of the groom choose their own wedding day dresses or gowns; however, the bride and groom may politely offer some suggestions. Some brides and grooms choose to set some guidelines when it comes to the gowns their mothers should wear. The couple may ask the mothers to wear full-length dresses or avoid certain colors. They also may ask the women to avoid patterns, or give them swatches of their color scheme so they can choose colors that match well.

The father of the bride and father of the groom might choose to wear the same suits or tuxedos as the groomsmen. This will eliminate the hassle of finding a matching suit and may save the couple the embarrassment of their fathers wearing old, outdated suits. However, the fathers will want to set themselves apart from the rest of the group. Again, this can be done with the same types of accessories worn by the groomsmen. A good option, however, is to choose accessories that will match well with their wives' wedding-day attire.

Guest Attire

You also have the responsibility of guiding your guests into wearing appropriate attire — attire that fits the formality and style of your wedding. The best way to handle this is to address it on the wedding invitation. For example, you might include a line that says, "formal attire," or "casual-chic attire." This alleviates embarrassment for your guests by them showing up dressed inappropriately.

Money-Saving Tips

Money-saving tip #1: When renting tuxedos, have everyone in the bridal party rent at the same place and at the same time. Most tuxedo shops offer a discount or a free tuxedo to the groom when the rest of the bridal party rents from the shop. The shop also might include a free ring bearer tuxedo that matches the groom's tuxedo.

Money-saving tip #2: Avoid tuxedos altogether. Allow the men in the bridal party to wear suits they already own.

Money-saving tip #3: Instead of picking one dress for the bridesmaids to wear, decide on a color. Allow each of the bridesmaids to choose her own dress, as long as it fits the chosen color and style (formal or informal).

Money-saving tip #4: Have the bridesmaids wear their own jewelry, accessories, and shoes.

Money-saving tip #5: Take a picture of the bridal gown or dress desired. Take the picture to a wedding dressmaker or seamstress. See if he or she can make the gown for less money than the shop is charging.

Money-saving tip #6: Borrow a wedding dress from a friend, family member, or coworker. Most brides only wear the dress once, so as long as it is dry-cleaned and the size you need, then you can cut out the expense of buying a wedding dress. If it is not your size, see if the dress owner will allow you to have it altered.

Money-saving tip #7: Buy floor models. Wedding dress shops typically have one sample of each of the dresses they sell. When the new styles come in, the dress shops need to sell the existing samples to make room. Typically, you can get the sample dresses at a discount. You will need to dry-clean and probably alter the dress. Check it for any stains or missing **embellishments**, so you know the other alterations you need to make and budget for before buying it.

Money-saving tip #8: Consignment shops can be a gold mine for wedding dresses, suits, and bridesmaid dresses. Brides often put the dresses up on consignment to recoup some of the money they spent on the gown. It is easy to find name-brand and high-end designer dresses at deeply discounted prices.

Money-saving tip #9: Check out bridal shops in a different part of town, city, or state. Affluent areas will have bloated prices on everything, including wedding gowns. Search for shops in middle-class areas, and you could see significant savings. Although it may not be easy to travel to another state, if you have friends or family spread around the country, you can have them do some shopping for you.

Money-saving tip #10: Attend designer trunk shows and sample sales — an amazing way to get your hands on a designer gown at a fraction of the cost. Look in bridal magazines, bridal websites, and in your newspaper's bridal inserts for dates and locations.

Money-saving tip #11: Major department stores normally have bridal departments that are likely to be less expensive, and they have amazing sales throughout the year. Call and find out when they normally mark down their bridal selection.

Money-saving tip #12: You can save money by purchasing your dress at an outlet store. The Yellow Pages and the Internet are great places to begin.

Money-saving tip #13: Newspaper and online classified ads are another place to find great deals. For whatever reason, many women decide to part with their wedding dress. You will be surprised at the bargains you can find.

You are dressed to impress and ready to go — down the aisle, that is. With the attire and accessory needs out of the way, it is now time to figure out transportation needs for the day of the wedding. *Chapter 15 helps you with the tips and advice to consider about providing transportation for the different members of the wedding party, including you, and what your different options are.*

CHAPTER FIFTEEN

Getting To and Fro

Now, it is time to go back to the logistical part of planning a wedding. Although flowers and music add nice touches and tend to be more of a

sentimental nature, the transportation of the bride, groom, and even the rest of the bridal party is an important aspect to the overall wedding plan that often is overlooked. The wedding day tends to be a hectic one, so transportation plays a vital role in ensuring everyone is where they need to be when they need to be there. In this chapter, you will learn about all the transportation needs to consider. You also will find some money-saving tips to help with the wedding budget.

Bride Transportation to the Ceremony

The wedding cannot start until the bride arrives, so one of the most important details to consider is how you will get to the ceremony location. Traditionally, the bride and her father, or the person escorting the bride down the aisle, arrive together. This way, the ceremony can start promptly. You have a few different options for arranging transportation to the ceremony. If the ceremony venue is where you will be getting ready, you might arrange to ride with one of your bridesmaids and have your father or escort meet you later. When the bride is making a grand entrance, you should consider renting a limousine, old car, carriage, or some kind of transportation to pull up to the ceremony.

Groom Transportation to the Wedding

Many couples choose to make transportation arrangements for the groom and his groomsmen. This is especially true if you want to ensure the groom, and his side of the bridal party, arrive for the ceremony on time. Limousines, stretch Hummers®, and old cars are some of the favorite transportation options for the guys. Some car rental and transportation agencies specialize in classic cars. Most transportation companies include modern and classic luxury vehicles, such as a vintage Rolls Royce. Some rental agencies charge more than the traditional rental fee because it is a classic or vintage vehicle. These rental agencies or transportation companies often rent these vehicles out for weddings, so they tend to offer packages to help keep the option at a cost-effective rate.

Wedding Party Transportation

Another option is to rent a limousine, small bus, or something big enough to hold the entire wedding party — guys and girls. Again, this ensures your bridal party arrives at the ceremony venue on time and is ready to go when you and the groom are. The same transportation can take the entire bridal party from the ceremony to the reception location, if the venues are different.

If your children are part of the wedding, arrange for dressing the children and bringing them to the wedding as well. Older children should be able to dress themselves, but make sure they are able to ride in the bridal party transportation or that someone is responsible for driving them. For smaller children, such as babies and toddlers, arrange for a family member or friend to take the children for the day. Leave their clothing and accessories with the caretaker to dress them and bring them to the ceremony. These should be the same people responsible for caring for young children during the ceremony and the reception. If you intend to leave for your honeymoon right after the reception, it might be easier to make the same people responsible for taking care of the children while you are away.

Getting the Bride and Groom from Ceremony to Reception

If you hire a ride to the church for the bride and the escort, this same vehicle can transport the bride and groom from the ceremony to the reception location. This allows you and your new spouse to spend a few minutes of quiet time together between the chaos of the ceremony and the chaos of the reception.

Another idea is to use a horse-drawn carriage. In true Cinderella and Prince Charming style, the bride and groom might be picked up from the church like they are royalty and driven to the reception location. Rural areas tend to offer this option: You could rent the horse and carriage and hire a driver from one of the local farms that offers a horse-drawn carriage as a service. Some large cities, such as New York City that is known for offering horse-drawn carriage rides in Central Park, also have local companies that rent the horses, carriage, and a driver for weddings.

You can allow your imagination to run wild when it comes to transportation. For example, you might associate the form of transportation with one of your professions or hobbies. This could land you in the seat of a fire truck next to your fireman husband with the sirens blaring. It also could put you both in the cockpit of a race car to race from the church to the wedding reception or from the reception off to your honeymoon.

Heading to the Honeymoon

The same transportation that brought the bride and groom to the reception also can carry them off for their honeymoon or the wedding night. Another option is to drop one of your cars off at the reception venue ahead of time. If you decide to do this, then you and your groom can drive off into the sunset (or other time of the day) on your own. If you intend on drinking alcohol at the reception, consider having someone drive you, a professional or even someone you know, so you do not encounter any legal problems as you head off to start your new life together.

Destination Wedding Transportation

For destination weddings, especially when you have many guests coming from out of the state/country, it is a nice option to rent a bus to take the guests from the hotel to the wedding location. You might even want to arrange shuttle-type transportation from the airport to the hotel when guests first arrive at the destination wedding location. This alleviates the necessity of each guest having to rent a vehicle and drive in a foreign country. If the destination wedding is in the United States, you still can choose to rent some form of transportation to make it easy for your guests to get to and from the wedding. Guests always have the option of making their own transportation arrangements. You also could think about providing this service if most of your guests are staying at one hotel, and you do not want them driving home after consuming alcohol at the wedding reception.

Questions to Ask the Transportation Services

If you have decided to splurge and rent some limousines, classic cars, or other types of transportation to whisk you and your bridal party from location to location, you will want to choose this

service as carefully as you have chosen each vendor so far. As you meet with different transportation providers, be sure you have answers to all of your questions. Having all of the answers allows you to make an educated decision when choosing the type of transportation for your wedding day and the type of transportation to best fit your needs.

Ask the following questions to any services you are considering:

- What car types and sizes are available? How many people can fit comfortably into each type and size?

- What amenities are included with the price, and which cost extra?

- Do they offer a wedding discount package? For rental companies that do, you might get a free bottle of champagne or another congratulatory gift.

- If you are renting a limo, are they a member of the National Limousine Association? Check them out at **www.limo.org**.

- If you need more than one car, will you receive a discount for each additional rental?

- Does the fee come with a set amount of miles and gas, or is that an extra fee?

- Will you need a driver? What will the driver wear? Unless your wedding is ultra casual, you do not want the chauffeur showing up in jeans and a T-shirt.

- Are you able to review their operating license and insurance certificate?

Money-Saving Tips

Money-saving tip #1: Consider packages. Compare the package pricing for transportation to the hourly rate. If you intend to hire transportation to drop everyone off at the ceremony and then take them to the reception, packages are typically more cost effective. If you only arrange for one-way transportation, then hourly pricing might be more cost effective.

Money-saving tip #2: Use one transportation company for all your needs. Most companies offer discounts when you hire more than one vehicle.

Money-saving tip #3: Rent a fancy car and drive yourselves. For an inexpensive rental fee, you can rent the car of your dreams. You and the groom can drive yourselves to the ceremony, if you do not care about seeing each other before the ceremony, or simply drive the car away from the reception.

Money-saving tip #4: Get a friend with a cool car to drive you. If someone you know owns a car, such as an old '65 Corvette convertible, Ferrari, or an old Rolls Royce, ask if they are willing to be your driver or if you can borrow the car. In this case, your only cost would be the gas.

Money-saving tip #5: Forgo offering transportation or hiring vehicles altogether. Simply have everyone be responsible for their own transportation to and from the ceremony and reception.

Money-saving tip #6: If you or someone you know owns a boat and the venue is on the water, make a watery getaway.

Money-saving tip #7: Borrow or use your own horse and carriage, or just the horse, and ride away on horseback.

With the need to get to and fro out of the way, you can leave the logistical parts of planning the wedding behind and get back into the more fun aspects of wedding planning — more parties. The wedding ceremony and reception typically are not the only celebrations you have to mark your unity. *In Chapter 16, learn about some of the other celebrations and parties leading up to your big day.*

Other Wedding Celebrations

What about all of the other parties and celebrations that come along with being a bride and groom-to-be? Should you really have to miss all of the fun just because it is not your first wedding? The short answer to the question is no, you do not and should not miss any and all of the other parties and celebrations that come along with getting married — first time or no.

Various parties typically lead up to the wedding. If the bride and groom are following etiquette, then some of these celebrations are not necessary. Planning these celebrations depends on the preference of couple. More second timers than not opt to have these celebrations. According to *Bride Again* magazine, 68 percent of second-time brides opt to participate in bridal showers and other wedding traditions and celebrations that some think are only for first timers.

Engagement Party

Once the ring is on the finger, you will want to share the engagement with everyone you know. It is completely acceptable for second brides and grooms to have an engagement party. You should, however, wait until all divorces are final. If one of you is still going through the legal proceedings of a divorce, hold off on having any wedding celebrations. A friend or family member should host the engagement party once one is scheduled.

Traditionally, an engagement party is a celebration that represents the formal announcement of the engagement. Some engagement-party hosts hold the celebration at home while others choose to rent a banquet hall, ballroom at a hotel, area at a bed and breakfast, or other rental venue. The party typically has refreshments, including champagne for the toast given by the hosts. The best man and maid of honor, as well as the parents of the bride and groom, also might opt to give toasts. Most engagement parties also have a cake to serve as dessert after the meal or the appetizers.

For a second wedding engagement party, the couple might wish to throw the party themselves, but according to etiquette, the couple should not throw their own engagement party. Gifts are appropriate at the engagement

party. Couples might also request that guests donate money to the couple's favorite charity or forgo gifts altogether.

Another thing to keep in mind is that anyone who is invited to the engagement party, according to etiquette, also must be invited to the wedding. In other words, couples should not use the engagement party as a way to incorporate guests in the wedding that the couple will not be able to incorporate on the wedding day itself.

Wedding Shower

To shower or not to shower the second time around, that is the question? Etiquette says it is perfectly acceptable for a bride walking down the aisle for a second time to have a bridal shower. However, etiquette dictates that a wedding shower hostess is a friend or member of the bridal party, not the bride herself and not a member of the family.

When deciding on the wedding shower, the bride can work with the maid of honor to let her know what the bride wants, but it is etiquette for the maid of honor to host the party. The rest of the bridesmaids also can contribute to the planning.

Wedding shower options are abundant. For example, some maids of honor pick a theme for the shower and then coordinate all of the planning efforts, even the gifts, around the theme. Some theme examples include:

- **Lingerie:** A lingerie party hostess might come and model the different types of lingerie the company sells. Party guests can buy lingerie for their own wardrobes and buy lingerie for the bride-to-be.

An alternative is to have the guests buy and bring their own choice of lingerie without having a lingerie party host.

- **Kitchen:** Bring in a hostess that represents a kitchen company to show off the various cooking and baking products the company sells. Guests might buy supplies for their own kitchen as well as help the bride-to-be stock her new kitchen. An alternative is to have the guests buy and bring their own choice of kitchen items without having a kitchen party host.

- **Bath:** Tell guests to bring supplies to stock the couple's bathrooms. This might include standard bath towels, hand towels, and wash clothes. It also might include monogrammed towels and linens. Bath soaps, bubble bath, and body wash, as well as other décor for the bathroom, is also acceptable.

- **Basket:** Assign a theme basket to each guest. Have the guest fill this basket with items that relate to the basket theme. There might be a basket for each room in the house or hobbies the couple enjoys.

- **Luxury:** Host a luxurious day at the spa or bring in a spa company to pamper the shower guests. It might even be fun to have the guests give each other facials, manicures, and pedicures. Supply the beauty products and let everyone give each other a makeover.

- **Couples:** Many brides and grooms are bringing together the men and the women for a couples shower. In many circumstances, this is a party with refreshments and mingling but might or might not include games.

Another popular option at a bridal shower is the games. Games tend to be a staple for the shower, but the second time around, the bride may opt out of playing games. If games are on the agenda, some ideas to get the creative juices flowing include:

- **How well do you know each other?** This is a version of the newlywed game. The host and the bridal party should create a list of personal questions to ask the groom before the shower. He should provide the answers. At the party, the host asks the bride the same questions to see how many she gets right about her husband-to-be.

- **Dress the bride:** This is a form of project runway, where the guests are split up into small groups or teams. Each team is provided with a roll of toilet paper. They have to use the toilet paper to create a wedding dress of their own. Each group should consist of at least two to three people. One should be the "bride" and the other one or two people design the dress. Have a runway show where each of the team shows off their creation and vote on the best creation.

- **Adult Mad Libs:** Write a story about the bride or groom, but put in blank spaces where it indicates whether the writer should include a noun, pronoun, verb, adverb, adjective, or other type of word. Make a copy of the story and hand it out to each guest, or pair up the guests. Have one of the guests in the pair ask the other guest for the appropriate type of word. When they have filled in all the blanks, have each guest or pair read the story aloud.

Oftentimes, brides find themselves having multiple showers. Some brides-to-be have a shower thrown for them by their coworkers at work. In addition, their friends and family members might host a more personal shower away from the workplace. Do not be surprised if you have more than one person or group of people that wants to host a bridal shower for you.

Especially as it is your second time down the aisle, it is even common for a couples shower to prevail over a girls-only event. Couples showers are becoming more common because it allows the couple to share the big event with all of their friends and together, no matter whether their friends are guys or gals. A sit-down dinner at a restaurant, a brunch on the patio of someone's big home, or a luncheon at the club are all options for couples events to celebrate the wedding shower.

Bachelor and Bachelorette Parties

Again, whether the bride and groom heading down the aisle again opt to have bachelor and **bachelorette** parties is a preference of the couple. If the wedding is a first for either the bride or groom, then the tradition of having a bachelor or bachelorette party is part of the fun of getting married. Do not be afraid to think out of the box and let your maid of honor or best man know the type of bachelor or bachelorette party you want to have. It does not have to be the typical jaunt to the strip club or involve a stripper at all. Brides might opt for a getaway to the spa with their girlfriends, and the guys may plan a weekend getaway or an overnight stay at a local casino, at a lake house, or a beach house.

A second bride and groom might cut the party out, but it is not common to include children in these parties. These are adult parties by nature. Adult children may be included, depending on what the groom and his groomsmen, or bride and her bridesmaids, are doing for the party. If they are going to a strip club, then the adult son of the bride-to-be probably does not want to see the future husband of his mom getting a lap dance. If the party is a poker party, or something like that, then including an adult male child would be appropriate. The same holds true for inviting adult children to the bachelorette party.

The Rehearsal Dinner

Just because one or both of you have gone down the aisle before does not mean that you and your wedding party does not need to rehearse. It is perfectly standard to have a wedding ceremony rehearsal a day or two before the wedding. Afterward, the parents of the groom or the couple might host a special dinner for the bridal party. Traditionally, out-of-town guests also are invited to attend the rehearsal dinner if they are already in town for the wedding festivities.

The rehearsal dinner is usually a sit-down meal. The dinner might be hosted at a restaurant, or a caterer might provide the food at the host's home or a rented venue. Generally, the dinner attire depends  on the venue. If it is a formal restaurant, then dress attire is appropriate and probably required. If it is a barbecue on a farm, then theme attire, such as cowboy and cowgirl outfits might be worn, or casual clothing such as jeans is appropriate.

Traditionally, the parents of the groom pay for the rehearsal dinner. In a second wedding situation, a couple might pay for and host their own rehearsal dinner. Toasts are a common element for the rehearsal dinner, no matter the setting. The host of the dinner usually gives the toast before the meal starts. Some rehearsal dinners allow others to give toasts, especially important members of the family or close friends who will not be able to give a toast at the wedding.

On the other hand, how much practice do you need? If you are having a traditional wedding and you have both done it before, you might not need to rehearse. Generally, this is not the case because you are typically marrying at a different location that has different rules and ways of doing things. If, however, you opt to skip the rehearsal, you might also opt to skip the rehearsal dinner. Again, you can choose to be as traditional or nontraditional as you want to be. After all, it is your wedding.

Rehearsal Dinner Invitation List

You can use the following sheets to prepare your guest list for the rehearsal dinner. If someone else is hosting the dinner, such as the groom's parents, provide this list to them so they have all of the information they need to send out rehearsal dinner invitations. Formal invitations do not have to go in the mail. Email invitations or calling to invite guests to the dinner are both appropriate alternatives to traditional invitations.

Bride's Parents

Mother of the bride

Name: _____

Address: _____

Telephone: _____ Cell phone: _____

Response: _____

Father of the bride

Name: _____

Address: _____

Telephone: _____ Cell phone: _____

Response: _____

Bride's Siblings

Sibling

Name: _____

Address: _____

Telephone: _____ Cell phone: _____

Response: _____

Sibling

Name: _____

Address: _____

Telephone: _____ Cell phone: _____

Response: _____

Bride's Siblings

Sibling

Name: _____

Address: _____

Telephone: _____ Cell phone: _____

Response: _____

Sibling

Name: _____

Address: _____

Telephone: _____ Cell phone: _____

Response: _____

Bride's Grandparents

Grandmother of the bride

Name: _____

Address: _____

Telephone: _____ Cell phone: _____

Response: _____

Grandfather of the bride

Name: _____

Address: _____

Telephone: _____ Cell phone: _____

Response: _____

Bride's Grandparents

Grandmother of the bride

Name: _____

Address: _____

Telephone: _____ Cell phone: _____

Response: _____

Grandfather of the bride

Name: _____

Address: _____

Telephone: _____ Cell phone: _____

Response: _____

Bride's Godparents

Godmother of the bride

Name: _____

Address: _____

Telephone: _____ Cell phone: _____

Response: _____

Godfather of the bride

Name: _____

Address: _____

Telephone: _____ Cell phone: _____

Response: _____

Bride's Aunts and Uncles

Aunt of the bride

Name: _____

Address: _____

Telephone: _____ Cell phone: _____

Response: _____

Uncle of the bride

Name: _____

Address: _____

Telephone: _____ Cell phone: _____

Response: _____

Aunt of the bride

Name: _____

Address: _____

Telephone: _____ Cell phone: _____

Response: _____

Uncle of the bride

Name: _____

Address: _____

Telephone: _____ Cell phone: _____

Response: _____

Groom's Parents

Mother of the groom

Name: _____

Address: _____

Telephone: _____ Cell phone: _____

Response: _____

Father of the groom

Name: _____

Address: _____

Telephone: _____ Cell phone: _____

Response: _____

Groom's Siblings

Sibling

Name: _____

Address: _____

Telephone: _____ Cell phone: _____

Response: _____

Sibling

Name: _____

Address: _____

Telephone: _____ Cell phone: _____

Response: _____

Groom's Siblings

Sibling

Name: _____

Address: _____

Telephone: _____ Cell phone: _____

Response: _____

Sibling

Name: _____

Address: _____

Telephone: _____ Cell phone: _____

Response: _____

Groom's Grandparents

Grandmother of the groom

Name: _____

Address: _____

Telephone: _____ Cell phone: _____

Response: _____

Grandfather of the groom

Name: _____

Address: _____

Telephone: _____ Cell phone: _____

Response: _____

Groom's Grandparents

Grandmother of the groom

Name: _____

Address: _____

Telephone: _____   Cell phone: _____

Response: _____

Grandfather of the groom

Name: _____

Address: _____

Telephone: _____   Cell phone: _____

Response: _____

Bride's Godparents

Godmother of the groom

Name: _____

Address: _____

Telephone: _____   Cell phone: _____

Response: _____

Godfather of the groom

Name: _____

Address: _____

Telephone: _____   Cell phone: _____

Response: _____

Groom's Aunts and Uncles

Aunt of the groom

Name: _____

Address: _____

Telephone: _____ Cell phone: _____

Response: _____

Uncle of the groom

Name: _____

Address: _____

Telephone: _____ Cell phone: _____

Response: _____

Aunt of the groom

Name: _____

Address: _____

Telephone: _____ Cell phone: _____

Response: _____

Uncle of the groom

Name: _____

Address: _____

Telephone: _____ Cell phone: _____

Response: _____

Female Roles

Role: ❑ Maid of honor ❑ Bridesmaid ❑ Flower girl

Name: _____

Address: _____

Telephone: _____ Cell phone: _____

Response: _____

Role: ❑ Maid of honor ❑ Bridesmaid ❑ Flower girl

Name: _____

Address: _____

Telephone: _____ Cell phone: _____

Response: _____

Role: ❑ Maid of honor ❑ Bridesmaid ❑ Flower girl

Name: _____

Address: _____

Telephone: _____ Cell phone: _____

Response: _____

Role: ❑ Maid of honor ❑ Bridesmaid ❑ Flower girl

Name: _____

Address: _____

Telephone: _____ Cell phone: _____

Response: _____

Role: ❑ Maid of honor ❑ Bridesmaid ❑ Flower girl

Name: _____

Address: _____

Telephone: _____ Cell phone: _____

Response: _____

Role: ❑ Maid of honor ❑ Bridesmaid ❑ Flower girl

Name: _____

Address: _____

Telephone: _____ Cell phone: _____

Response: _____

Male Roles

Role: ❑ Best man ❑ Groomsman ❑ Usher ❑ Ring bearer

Name: _____

Address: _____

Telephone: _____ Cell phone: _____

Response: _____

Role: ❑ Best man ❑ Groomsman ❑ Usher ❑ Ring bearer

Name: _____

Address: _____

Telephone: _____ Cell phone: _____

Response: _____

Role: ❑ Best man ❑ Groomsman ❑ Usher ❑ Ring bearer

Name: _____

Address: _____

Telephone: _____ Cell phone: _____

Response: _____

Role: ❑ Best man ❑ Groomsman ❑ Usher ❑ Ring bearer

Name: _____

Address: _____

Telephone: _____ Cell phone: _____

Response: _____

Role: ❑ Best man ❑ Groomsman ❑ Usher ❑ Ring bearer

Name: _____

Address: _____

Telephone: _____ Cell Phone: _____

Response: _____

Role: ❑ Best man ❑ Groomsman ❑ Usher ❑ Ring bearer

Name: _____

Address: _____

Telephone: _____ Cell phone: _____

Response: _____

Wedding Service

Officiant

Name: _____

Address: _____

Telephone: _____ Cell phone: _____

Response: _____

Reader

Name: _____

Address: _____

Telephone: _____ Cell phone: _____

Response: _____

Musician

Name: _____

Address: _____

Telephone: _____ Cell phone: _____

Response: _____

Another etiquette faux pas second brides and grooms worry about is the gift registry. *Chapter 17 helps you decide whether to register for gifts and where to register.*

CHAPTER SEVENTEEN

Gift Registry

Giving and receiving gifts can leave both the giver and the receiver with a big smile on their faces, and weddings are one of the biggest gift-giving events that exist in our lives. Etiquette, however,  tries to put a little chink in the armor because it says that if both the bride and groom have been married before then the traditional gift registry is not proper. It does not say, however, that alternative gift registries are not proper. In modern times, brides and grooms are shunning gift registry etiquette and registering for the traditional pots, pans, and houseware items, as well as gifts they really want or need. This chapter covers when to establish a registry and what types of items to register for, depending on the situation.

To Register or Not to Register

Whether you choose to register for wedding gifts is up to you and your spouse-to-be. As a second time bride or groom, you might already have one or two functioning households, with pots, pans, dishware, silverware, and more. If this is not the case, then the modern etiquette book says that registering for gifts, even for a second wedding is perfectly acceptable. Registries are one of those touchy subjects that you might have to battle with opinions from friends and family members about. Although you should listen to opinions and consider what other people think, do not allow this to sway you too much in one direction or another. You might rightfully need and want to register for certain housewares and gifts to kick off your new life with your new spouse.

You can use the following registry checklist for a traditional store registry:

Registry Checklist			
Item	Qty.	Brand/Collection Name	Store
8-12 place settings			
Pasta bowls			
Accent plates			
Large vegetable bowls			
Serving bowls			
Casserole dishes			
Medium platters			
Large platters			
Gravy boat and stand			
Butter dish			
Sugar bowl			
Creamer			

(Formal Dinnerware)

Registry Checklist			
Item	Qty.	Brand/Collection Name	Store
Salt & pepper shakers			
Teapot			
Fine china storage			
8-12 place settings			
Serving spoons			
Serving meat fork			
Extra teaspoons			
Extra salad forks			
Pierced tablespoons			
Soup spoons			
Sugar spoon			
Butter spreader			
Silverware storage			
Water goblets			
Red wine glasses			
White wine glasses			
Champagne flutes			
Martini glasses			
Martini shaker			
Highball glasses			
Pilsner glasses			
Beer steins			
Brandy glasses			
Shot glasses			
Double Old-Fashioned glasses			

Categories (vertical labels): Formal Silver, Formal Crystal, Barware

Registry Checklist			
Item	Qty.	Brand/Collection Name	Store
8-12 place settings			
Pasta bowls			
Accent plates			
Cereal bowls			
Large vegetable bowls			
Serving bowls			
Casserole dishes			
Medium platters			
Large platters			
Gravy boat and stand			
Butter dish			
Sugar bowl			
Creamer			
Salt & pepper shakers			
Teapot			
8-12 place settings			
Soup spoons			
Serving set			
Hostess set			
Entertainment set			
Water goblets			
Red wine glasses			
White wine glasses			
Champagne flutes			
Tall beverage glasses			
Juice glasses			

Row groups (left margin labels): Everyday Dinnerware (8-12 place settings through Teapot); Everyday Silverware (8-12 place settings through Entertainment set); Everyday Glassware (Water goblets through Juice glasses).

Registry Checklist			
Item	Qty.	Brand/Collection Name	Store
Pilsner glasses			
Beer steins			
Sauce pans			
Sauté pans			
Stock pot/Dutch oven			
Steamer/double broiler			
Roasting pan			
Lasagna pan			
Casserole dishes			
Griddle			
Wok			
Omelet pan			
Toaster/toaster oven			
Blender			
Grill/griddle			
Waffle maker			
Coffee maker			
Cappuccino maker			
Bread maker			
Rice cooker/steamer			
Food processor			
Mixer			
Juicer			
Bread pans			
Muffin tins			
Pizza pans			
Cake pans			

Row groups (left margin labels): Cookware, Kitchen Appliances, Bakeware

Registry Checklist			
Item	Qty.	Brand/Collection Name	Store
Pie tins			
Casserole dishes			
Cookie sheets			
Roasting pans			
Knife block			
Cleaver			
Bread knife			
Paring knife			
Chef knife			
Carving knife			
Slicing knife			
Steak knives			
Knife sharpener			
Mixing bowls			
Measuring cups			
Measuring spoons			
Cooking utensils			
Serving utensils			
Meat thermometer			
Colander			
Canisters			
Trivet			
Hot pads			
Dish towels			

Cutlery

Kitchen Tools

Registry Checklist			
Item	Qty.	Brand/Collection Name	Store
Table Linens			
Tablecloth			
Table runner			
Place mats			
Napkins			
Napkin rings			
Bath Items			
Bath sheets			
Bath towels			
Hand towels			
Washcloths			
Shower curtain			
Shower curtain rings			
Shower curtain liner			
Bath rugs			
Toilet paper holder			
Hand towel bar			
Towel bar			
Toothbrush holder			
Soap holder			
Lotion dispenser			
Tissue holder			
Waste basket			
Grooming Kit			
Linens			
Comforter			
Duvet			
Quilt			
Pillow shams			
Flat sheets			

Registry Checklist			
Item	Qty.	Brand/Collection Name	Store
Fitted sheets			
Bed skirt			
Mattress pad			
Curtains			
Throw pillows			
Extra blankets			
Pillows			
Candlesticks			
Vases			
Frames			
Mirrors			
Throw pillows			
Lamps			

If you do not need the typical items new brides and grooms do to set up a new household, then you absolutely can sway from tradition. You can allow your creative juices to flow and register for items that you want more than you need. Modern brides and grooms are thinking out of the box and registering for gifts to receive the items they really want. For example, adventurous brides and grooms that love to ski might register at their favorite ski equipment and supplies store. A couple that would rather have their honeymoon paid for than receive a place setting for eight might register with a specialty travel site that allows their guests to chip in on paying for their honeymoon.

Types of Registries

Although the most common type of gift registry is for housewares, the only limit on what you can register for is where you allow your imagination to take you. To help you get your creative juices flowing, consider some of the other types of registries that are becoming increasingly common for brides and grooms the second time around:

- Wines from around the world — clubs, subscriptions, and wine delivery programs (Italian Wine Merchants **www.italianwinemerchants.com**)

- Hobbies, such as skiing, camping, or scuba diving (REI **www.rei.com**)

- Home improvement, such as Home Depot® (**www.homedepot.com**) or Lowe's® (**www.lowes.com**), for home improvement projects

- Luxury household items, such as an espresso machine, pasta maker, and other innovative kitchen gadgets (Bed Bath & Beyond®, Pier 1® Imports, Crate & Barrel, and Williams-Sonoma®)

- Art and decorative items for your new home

- Honeymoon (Honey Luna™: **www.honeyluna.com**)

- Museum memberships

- Family board games for family night in (Target, Bed Bath & Beyond, and other department and big box stores)

- Gift certificates to the couple's and family's favorite restaurants (not necessarily a registry, but a gift option for couples that do not want traditional household goods)

- Movie tickets (not necessarily a registry, but a gift option for couples that do not want traditional household goods)

Although these are few jumping points for you to start thinking out of the box, this certainly is not where your gift registries end. Come up with some ideas of your own, and then sit down with your partner and get his or ideas down on paper, too. Nothing is too far-fetched. If you come up with an idea, find a website or store that allows you to register for the items or services you are interested in receiving as wedding gifts.

Registry Alternatives

If you are the type of bride and groom that would rather give to others than receive, you have options in this arena, too. In lieu of wedding gifts of any kind, some couples are asking wedding guests to contribute the money they would normally spend on a gift to the couple's favorite cause or charity, or the guest's favorite cause or charity, in the name of the couple.

Another option is to combine gift giving and charity. Organizations, such as the I Do Foundation® (**www.idofoundation.org**) contribute a percentage of the price of the wedding gift to the chosen charity or cause. A similar site is Just Give (**www.justgive.org**), which also allows wedding guests to shop at hundreds of stores for your wedding gifts and contribute a percentage of their purchases to one of over a million charities and causes.

Once you decide to register or not to register, then you have to decide where to register and what to register for. With this out of the way, it is time to get on to planning the real fun of a wedding — the honeymoon or "familymoon."

CHAPTER EIGHTEEN

The Honeymoon

After all the stress of planning a wedding weighing on your shoulders, brides and grooms often head off on a honeymoon to relax and take some time to start their new life together on a romantic and relaxing foot. When it is a second honeymoon for second wedding, the bride and groom have options. Some couples choose to head off on their honeymoon alone, while others make it a family affair and take the children, which has earned the term "familymoon."

Just the Two of You

The most common type of honeymoon is, of course, the two of you jetting off to a destination of your choice for some rest and relaxation. Traditionally, the groom is responsible for planning and paying for the honeymoon. In modern times, however, couples are planning their getaway together. In some cases, grooms want to surprise the bride, so they keep the tradition alive. Some popular honeymoon destinations include:

- Mexico
- Caribbean islands

- Cruises
- Jamaica
- Aruba
- Spain
- Italy

One thing you want to think about if you decide to go it alone is making arrangements for someone to take care of your kids at home while you are gone. Ideally, the other parent should step in for the job, but if this is not possible, find a friend or family member who can take over your parental duties while you are gone. Whatever you do, choose someone the kids enjoy being with because the kids will be going through enough emotions with a new stepfamily to deal with without having to deal with being left with a crabby aunt or neighbor that they despise.

Younger children might have a hard time understanding what a honeymoon is and why their mom or dad is leaving them behind. As the parent, you should sit down with your children to explain your trip. Let them know that you are going on vacation with your new spouse, but that you will be back. You might think of marking the time you will be gone on the calendar. Tell the child to mark an "X" in the day each night before he or she goes to bed, so he or she will be able to visualize when you are coming back and even count down the days. If you intend on having a family vacation after the honeymoon or at some point later when you will be taking all of the kids with you, let them know this as well. A trip in the future gives the children something to look forward to and focus on, so that it takes the sting out of you being away from them.

For couples that have chosen a destination wedding, you might combine the wedding and the honeymoon destination into one. Keep in mind, however, that if you have guests at a destination wedding, they might turn the trip into a vacation of their own, so you should consider ensuring you are staying at different resorts, hotels, or cities if you want your alone time together without running into family members and friends.

Questions you should ask yourself to help choose your honeymoon options:

- What is your budget?
- How long will you be gone?
- Do you want to travel somewhere new?
- What type of climate do you want?
- What activities would you like to do?
- Is there anywhere you have always dreamed of visiting?

Packing for your Honeymoon

Packing for your honeymoon ultimately depends on where you are planning on going and how long you will be there. These lists are guidelines, but they will make you think about the things you need to pack and items you might have forgotten about. Try to start your shopping and packing several weeks before your wedding. Everything is going to get hectic quickly, so try to get everything done as early as possible. Make sure to check all guidelines as to what can and cannot be brought on a plane or into another country. In many cases, items such as shampoo and toothpaste only can be in certain size bottles if placed in your carry-on.

Important documents you will need (put all the papers together in a manila envelope):

- Airline tickets, tickets for any events or shows
- Confirmation and deposit information emails and letters from airlines, hotels, restaurants, and activities you have planned
- Passports/visas/driver's licenses/copies of birth certificates
- Telephone numbers for your travel agent, doctors, house/pet sitter/babysitter, veterinarian, and credit card companies
- Health insurance and prescription cards
- Credit cards and traveler's checks
- Luggage tags and locks
- Prescription medications (in the original bottles)

Items you likely will use:

- Camera
- Toothpaste
- Toothbrushes
- Mouthwash
- Deodorant
- Body wash
- Shampoo

- Conditioner
- Soap
- Comb and brush
- Razors
- Shaving cream
- Aftershave
- Nail files
- Nail clippers
- Tweezers
- Hair accessories
- Lotion
- Contact lens care items
- Clothing, bras, underwear, socks, lingerie, pajamas, bathrobes, shoes, and any other necessities for the number of days that you will be away

Other items to consider:

- Sunscreen
- Sunglasses
- Hats
- Insect repellent
- Pain relievers
- Antihistamines
- Common medicines to help with common illnesses, such as motion sickness, diarrhea, constipation, or acid reflux
- Antibacterial lotions/soaps
- Bandages
- Feminine hygiene products
- Electrical adapters

- Alarm clock
- Tote bag or small backpacks
- Guidebook
- Sewing kit
- Safety pins

Items in your carry-on bag:

- Snacks
- Books
- Magazines
- Jewelry
- Laptop
- Deck of cards
- Light clothing
- Eye mask
- Earplugs

Items to leave behind for others:

- Flight numbers, arrival and departure times
- Your itinerary
- Telephone numbers of all hotels
- Copies of receipts for traveler's checks
- Doctor's information and health cards for children
- Telephone numbers for police, fire department, and poison control for house sitters and babysitters
- Vet information for pet sitter
- Copies of your wills, life insurance, and financial information

A Family Vacation

You also could consider a family getaway with all of the kids included. This is an especially good idea if the children are struggling to wrap their minds around their new stepfamily. Rather than feed this apprehension by leaving them behind for a week or two, a "familymoon" might be the solution for finally bringing together your two families and helping them to form into one.

When the children are still young, a popular familymoon destination is Disney®. Disney in Orlando, Florida, or in California both offer family fun for every age. The adults have their own forms of entertainment they can enjoy at night with an in-room babysitter for the kids. During the day, the family can spend time at one or more of the many parks Disney offers.

Another great idea for a familymoon is a cruise. Cruise ships, such as Disney, cater to families. All of the activities onboard focus on children of all ages, including being able to visit with the Disney characters and much more. Regular cruises also have a day camp for kids, and activities for kids at night, so the parents can enjoy the adult activities onboard the ship.

When considering a family vacation, search for destinations that cater to families and cater to the age groups of your kids. Still consider your budget, and ask yourself the same questions you ask yourself when choosing a honeymoon spot. For example, many cruise lines have camp and activities for children, so the adults can enjoy the adult activities available as well. Even hotels and resorts offer babysitting services, so you and your new spouse can enjoy some time out on the town alone.

When you are planning a familymoon, this is an opportunity to bring the children in to help you choose the destination and even plan the trip. Have each of the children pick a place they would like to spend the vacation or present two or three options from which the children can choose. Hold a vote for the final destination with the majority ruling where the family spends the familymoon. Of course, do your research up front to ensure the places you offer as options fit your budget and are realistic vacation spots for the family.

When you are planning the sleeping arrangements, consider having children of similar ages room together. Book hotel rooms with adjoining doors, or consider renting a suite with enough bedrooms and pullout couches to accommodate everyone. Another option is to rent a vacation rental home, condo, cabin, or cottage with enough space to fit everyone from both families.

If there are two families of kids, the familymoon might be a prime opportunity to start melding to two families into one. If this is the first attempt to meld into one family, there might be some disagreements and tension between some of the children. These moments also are teaching opportunities for you as parents. Have a family meeting to discuss the issues when they arise and talk about how to resolve the problems. Enlist suggestions from the children on how they think they can resolve the problem, with you and your new spouse as the final decision makers on what the resolution is and how the rules stand for the future.

Although a familymoon provides the perfect opportunity to have some fun while also turning two families into one family, the ages of the children play a pivotal role in how well this will work. For example, if you have a baby or toddler, it might not be a good an idea to bring him or her on the familymoon. He or she will probably not be as affected by the changing family and might be a lot of trouble on a trip. Families with older children and teens, however, might find a familymoon beneficial for the new family, while still giving the new couple some happy alone time, too.

Money-Saving Tips

Money-saving tip #1: Negotiate a honeymoon stay at the hotel where you are hosting your wedding. Many hotels offer a complimentary honeymoon suite for the wedding night when the couple holds their reception at the hotel. You might even be able to negotiate a special rate for the rest of your stay.

Money-saving-tip #2: Book your travel arrangements, hotel stays, and excursions online. It is typically less expensive to book the arrangements online than by phone.

Money-saving tip #3: Look for package deals. It also tends to be less expensive to book package travel deals and honeymoon packages than to book the air travel, hotel stay, and rental car individually.

Money-saving tip #4: Bid on a vacation rental. Auction websites, such as eBay, and online classified ads, such as Craigslist, allow you to find vacation rentals. These vacation rentals tend to be fully equipped condos, houses, cottages, and cabins. With fully equipped kitchens, Jacuzzis, washers and dryers, and other amenities, it can save money to book a honeymoon stay where you can cook some of your meals and do laundry, so you do not have to pack as many clothes. Locations include beaches, mountains, lakes, and other romantic locations for a honeymoon experience. This is also a great option when choosing a familymoon because it saves money from renting multiple hotel rooms and always having to eat meals out.

Money-saving tip #5: Plan a trip that fits the budget. Although two weeks in Europe might be your ideal honeymoon, it might be too much for your bank accounts. Opt to drive across country or visit a domestic location for a week or two instead. Choose locations that offer excursions, restaurants, and other amenities that you can enjoy together as a couple.

Money-saving tip #6: Search for all-inclusive resorts and packages. All-in-one resorts allow you to pay a flat price per person. The flat rate typically includes the room, food, and beverages. Some packages even include excursions and extracurricular activities.

Money-saving tip #7: Do a home swap. Yes, similar to the movie, there are people in other countries and other states willing to swap homes with you for a week or two. You might be able to get a fully equipped home in Europe for the price that you would normally pay for a hotel room stay in the states. Look for websites specifically set up for home swapping. Also, search classified advertisements online. You even can contact reputable real estate agents that specialize in these types of vacation homes. Be careful of scams, and if someone asks you to wire money, check into the legitimacy of the company handling the transaction before doing anything of the sort. Swapping homes, essentially, gives you a free place to stay, so all you have to pay for is the transportation to get there, food, drinks, and any activities you want to participate in during your stay.

Conclusion

So, there you have it. You are now ready to join the ranks of the second (third, fourth, or beyond) brides and grooms around the world. And, with all of the great information, advice, and tips you have picked up along the way, you can do it with your head held high and with style and grace. You now have all of the information you need to take your walk down the aisle for the second time and to do it in the style of your choice. You now know how to get over the emotional loss of a spouse or your divorce and

leave the sense of guilt or betrayal toward your first spouse behind. You now should be ready to move on and have the happiness you deserve. In other words, you are now ready to plan a great big celebration and party!

Take the lessons from your first marriage, and apply them toward making your second chance a better one. With your focus being to treat your second marriage as a separate sanctity than your first, you are ready to start the planning process with a fresh viewpoint — a viewpoint that just might be a lot more fun and festive than it was the first time around.

You now have learned how to approach planning your second wedding, such as dealing with your feelings about your first wedding and telling your children, your ex, and your ex-family members you are tying the knot again. In addition, you now know your choices of wedding styles. If sticking to etiquette is important to you, you have discovered some of the etiquette and feelings about planning a second wedding versus a first wedding and how to overcome each of these issues. You have all of the practical advice you need on budgeting, choosing venues, saving money, and tips, tricks, and advice from professional wedding planners and other professionals in the industry, and from those second brides and grooms that have gone down the aisle before you. You also have the checklists, planning worksheets, and sample ideas to help you get and stay organized throughout the planning process. So, go forth and plan!

Glossary

arm bouquet: A triangular-shaped bouquet held in your hand and up to the crook of your arm, it is popularly seen by winners of beauty pageants but is also a good choice for a bridal bouquet.

ascot: A type of bow tie that men wear during a daytime wedding ceremony. This particular bow tie has a wider tie than other tie options.

bachelorette: Bachelorette is the term used for the bride-to-be. The most common use of the term is for the bachelorette party, which is the last party the bride-to-be, her bridesmaids, and her girlfriends hold to celebrate being single before she walks down the aisle.

bridal shower: The bridal shower is a party where the bride-to-be, her friends, and family celebrate her upcoming nuptials. In more modern times, couples are choosing to throw the bridal shower together rather than have a girls-only party.

butter cream: Butter cream is a type of icing for the wedding cake. It has a whipped appearance and a creamy taste, which is different from the smooth and hard-like shell of fondant icing.

bow tie: A type of tie worn by the men in the wedding party. A short tie that knots against the throat of the wearer, its short tails stick out to the left and the right of the knot.

best man: The best man is the witness that stands up for the groom. He is responsible for signing the marriage certificate as the witness that the couple has entered into the marriage willingly. Traditionally, the best man also has other duties, such as throwing the bachelor party, helping the groom with his duties for the wedding and giving a speech or toast at the wedding reception.

boutonniere: A single flower or small cluster of flowers worn on the lapel of the men's suit or tuxedo jacket.

bride's bouquet: The arrangement of flowers the bride carries down the aisle. Typically, the bride's bouquet is bigger than the bridesmaids' flower bouquets and even might be different than the bouquets the bridesmaids carry.

candelabra: A decorative piece that holds candles. These decorative pieces come in different sizes and designs. Some are tall and can be used to line the aisle of the ceremony location, while others are smaller and made to stand on tables as centerpieces.

cascade: A cascading bridal bouquet is often a large bouquet that includes greenery and flowers that taper off. These can be quite heavy, so it is important to consider you will be holding this bouquet for your photographs.

chuppah: A canopy in a Jewish wedding where the bride and groom have the wedding ceremony. The chuppah is a symbol of their new home and of God.

cummerbund: A sash that men wear around their waists when wearing a tuxedo. Typically, the cummerbund matches the tie.

cutaway: This is the traditional morning coat. The swallowtail lines on the cutaway will be attractive on almost any frame. This is an excellent choice if the groomsmen are of varied heights and body shapes.

dinner jacket: The dinner jacket may be worn with formal trousers. It is more casual and can be worn in white or cream. Typically, it is worn with a necktie. It is acceptable in the afternoon or evening and is appropriate for summer weddings, destination weddings, or other warm-climate weddings.

double-breasted: A double-breasted jacket can effectively camouflage a larger-sized groom or groomsman. Things to look for: Make sure the size is correct, and try on several different cuts/styles to find the right one.

dyeables: Shoes made of a fabric that can be dyed to match the color of a dress. Most commonly, dyeables are worn by bridesmaids but also can be worn by brides or other members of the wedding party.

embellishments: Adornment and decorations, typically added to the wedding dress. Embellishments are also common elements in wedding stationery.

familymoon: A modern and commonly used term to describe a family vacation that takes place when a bride and groom that have children from previous marriages or relationships take the entire family with them on their honeymoon.

favors: Small mementos the bride and groom give their wedding guests to remember their wedding day.

fondant: A type of smooth and somewhat tasteless cake icing. This type of icing is draped over the cake rather than spread on with a knife.

guest book: A memory book wedding guests sign to give their well wishes to the couple.

garter: A stretchy band the bride wears around one of her legs, under her dress but over her stockings. At the reception, the groom removes the garter and tosses it to the eligible bachelors during the garter toss ceremony.

groom's cake: A cake separate from the wedding cake served at the wedding reception. The groom's cake typically offers a different dessert option for those that do not like the flavor of the wedding cake. The groom's cake is also a symbol of something the groom enjoys, such as a cake in the shape of a mascot, of a favorite hobby, or something else that represents the groom's personality.

hand-tied bouquet: A hand-tied bouquet is just as it sounds. The stems of the flowers are all left in the open and the bouquet is tied, either with a ribbon or greenery.

high vest: This style works best on men who are not broad in their upper torso. For men who are broad in this area but really want this style, the vest should be in a muted shade for the best look. If your groom is on the slender side, he can do anything he wants with patterns and colors.

low vest: Low vests are attractive on almost all body types. Just as with the high vest, broad men should go for muted shades, while smaller men can be freer with patterns and colors.

maid of honor: The maid of honor is the witness that stands up for the bride. She is responsible for signing the marriage certificate that the couple has entered into the marriage willingly. Traditionally, the maid of honor also has other duties, such as throwing the bachelorette party, helping the bride with her duties for the wedding and giving a speech or toast at the wedding reception.

mandarin/banded collar: For men with a thicker, shorter neck, this collar will not work well. A lay-down collar would be a better choice.

morning suit: A morning suit is for formal, morning weddings. Traditionally, it has a single button at the waist and a single tail in the back. It should be either black or grey and is worn with striped suit trousers.

nosegays: These are perfectly round bouquets, and even though they have been around for centuries, they are making a comeback in popularity. The size of the nosegay can range from small to large.

officiant: The person responsible for performing the wedding ceremony. The officiant typically is used when it is not a religious figure or religious ceremony, but a nondenominational wedding ceremony.

organza: A sheer material made of silk.

peaked lapel: The peaked tuxedo lapel is a great choice for shorter men, as it will make the body appear longer because it draws the eye up and out, creating length. This is also a good choice for taller men.

place cards: Small tent-like cards that tell wedding guests where to sit during the reception.

place setting: The pieces of dinnerware and silverware for each diner at the table. A complete place setting consists of a dinner plate, charger, soup bowl, bread-and-butter plate, salad fork, dinner fork, dessert fork, butter spreader, dinner knife, teaspoon, soupspoon, napkin, water goblet, red wine glass, and white wine glass. Typically, the place setting is a concern of the bride when she is registering for gifts. A place setting is also a concern when arranging with the catering company or rental company to obtain the dishes necessary for the wedding reception.

pocket square: Small handkerchief or piece of cloth stuffed into the jacket pocket of a suit. The pocket square is typically a replacement of the boutonniere.

processional: The formal walking of the bridal party down the aisle to start the wedding ceremony.

shawl collar: Shawl collars come in a variety of widths, and this makes them difficult to adhere to a certain body shape. Pay attention to the width and to the lines of the tux itself, and just try your eye.

single-blossom bouquet: Some brides choose to carry a single flower with them down the aisle. This simplicity can be stunning.

single-breasted (one- or two-button): This is the most classic of all tux jackets and will look terrific on most body shapes. Taller men should go for a two-button jacket, while shorter men should go for the one-button. The more shirt that shows means it creates a longer visual line, so shorter men should use that style to add the appearance of height.

single-breasted (three- or four-button): This is an ultra-popular jacket. These high-buttoning jackets are amazing on tall, slender men. Heavier men should consider the one- or two-button version.

suit: The standard suit is the attire of choice for a casual wedding.

tails: Tails are quite formal and are worn with suspenders and a bow tie. This is about as formal as a tuxedo gets. Unfortunately, this style sometimes can be unflattering on short or heavy men. It really depends on the length of their legs, as even short men can look great in tails.

tiara: A crown, usually made of jewels, the bride wears as a headpiece in place of or in addition to her veil.

toss bouquet: A small bouquet that sometimes resembles the bride's bouquet. The toss bouquet is the flower arrangement the bride throws to the crowd of single women at the wedding reception.

tulle: A material commonly used in weddings. It has a net-like appearance, but consists of nylon, silk, and rayon. It is a common material for veils and skirt overlays.

tuxedo or black tie: A formal jacket and slacks worn by the men in a wedding ceremony for a formal wedding. Most often black or grey, there are many styles to choose from, with different buttons and lapels. By tradition, these are worn only in the evening, but they can be acceptable at any time of the day.

unity candle: The lighting of the candle symbolizes the joining of the two separate families — the bride's family and the groom's family — into one family.

usher: A member or members of the wedding party responsible for escorting wedding guests to their seats for the wedding ceremony.

veil: A material piece the bride wears attached to her headpiece. The veil typically covers the bride's face as she comes down the aisle and is flipped over her head during the ceremony.

vendor: The general term used to describe the professionals that help you put together your wedding. These professionals include florists, decorators, venues, photographers, and all of the other companies you need to acquire the services and items you need for your wedding.

venue: Location of the wedding ceremony and/or the wedding reception.

vows: The bride and groom exchange statements to each other during the wedding ceremony as a symbol of their commitment and loyalty to each other.

vest: Attire worn by the men in the wedding ceremony that covers their shirt and waistband.

whipped cream: A light and less rich tasting icing than butter cream icing. This type of icing is the least expensive of the three finishing options. Whipped cream icing melts in heat or humid climates, and it does not lend itself well to many types of decorations.

Resources

Here are some resources you can turn to in helping plan your wedding. Some specifically relate to planning a wedding for the second bride and/or groom. Others are general wedding planning websites and resources that can help you plan any type of wedding.

Wedding Planning and Wedding Styles

These are some general wedding planning websites to turn to for almost any of your wedding planning needs.

- The Knot (**www.theknot.com**)
- Today's Bride (**www.todaysbride.com**)
- Wedding Channel (**www.weddingchannel.com**)
- Wed Plan (**www.wedplan.com**)
- Wedding Themes (**www.weddingthemes.com**)
- Bride Again Magazine (**www.brideagain.com**)

Invitations and Wedding Stationery

Here are a few wedding invitation resources for getting an idea on the style and type of invitations you want to order for your second wedding. Some sites allow you to order directly from the manufacturer. Other websites require you to find a dealer to place your order.

- Anna Griffin Invitation Design (**www.annagriffin.com**)
- Crane's (**www.crane.com**)
- Paper Style (**www.paperstyle.com**)

Flowers

These website resources provide general information on flowers. In addition, you can find florists in your area that are members of the organizations and associations to help as a starting point.

- American Institute of Floral Designers (**www.aifd.org**)
- Society of American Florists (**www.aboutflowers.com**)
- California Cut Flower Commission (**www.ccfc.org**)

Entertainment

Whether you are searching for a DJ or a live band for your wedding, these websites can help you narrow down your options. In addition, these websites offer educational resources and information on choosing professional entertainment and compiling a song list.

- American Federation of Musicians (**www.afm.org**)

- American Disc Jockey Association (**www.adja.org**)
- Pro DJ (**www.prodj.com**)

Photographers and Videographers

These associations and organizations help you to identify professional photographers and videographers that work in the area where your wedding is taking place.

- Wedding and Event Videographers Association (**www.weva.com**)
- Professional Photographers of America (**www.ppa.com**)

Transportation

Hitch a ride by using this organization to help you pinpoint reputable transportation companies in your local wedding area.

- National Limousine Association (**www.limo.org**)

Registry

Set up your gift registry and manage everything online. Many of these websites allow you to register for gifts from the comfort of your own home. Others allow you to combine an in-store visit with an online visit to complete your wedding gift registry.

- Bed Bath & Beyond (**www.bedbathandbeyond.com**)
- Crate & Barrel (**www.crateandbarrel.com**)

- Home Depot (**www.homedepot.com**)

- Pier 1 Imports (**www.pier1.com**)

- The Gift (**www.thegift.com**)

- REI (**www.rei.com**)

- Williams-Sonoma (**www.williams-sonoma.com**)

- The Honeymoon (**www.thehoneymoon.com**)

- Wine (**www.wine.com**)

- Wine of the Month Club (**www.winemonthclub.com**)

Second Brides and Grooms/Stepfamilies

These resources are specifically for encore brides and grooms — those walking down the aisle for a second time. The resources, information, tips, and advice speak directly to the issues that arise when marrying for the second time.

- I Do Take Two (**www.idotaketwo.com**)

- Second Wives café (**www.secondwivescafe.com**)

- The Second Wives Club (**www.secondwivesclub.com**)

Appendices

～ A P P E N D I X   A ～

Preliminary Planning Worksheet

This worksheet provides you with a complete overview of the wedding process you are about to tackle. Use this worksheet first to get your basic thoughts and intentions together. As you start the planning process, you will have a foundation and bases from which to build. Keep in mind your plans might change and transform over time.

PRELIMINARY PLANNING WORKSHEET	
Wedding Description	**Location**
❑ Formal	❑ Your home
❑ Informal	❑ Bride's hometown
❑ Traditional	❑ Groom's hometown
Wedding Style	**Preference**
❑ Nontraditional	❑ Other location
❑ Casual	❑ Indoor ceremony
❑ Festive	❑ Outdoor ceremony
❑ Religious	❑ Church – religious
❑ Contemporary	❑ Other – non-religious
Wedding Size	**Season**
❑ Intimate (fewer than 50)	❑ Spring
❑ Small (50 to 125)	❑ Summer

❑ Medium (125 to 250)	❑ Autumn
❑ Large (more than 250)	❑ Winter
Hour of Day	**Color Palette**
❑ Sunrise	❑ Pastels
❑ Midday	❑ Rich hues (jewel tones)
❑ Sunset	❑ All white
❑ Evening	❑ Black and white
❑ Late night	❑ Bright hues (primary colors)
Bride's Priorities	**Groom's Priorities**
❑ Season	❑ Season
❑ Location	❑ Location
❑ Guest list	❑ Guest List
❑ Type of ceremony	❑ Type of ceremony
❑ Reception location	❑ Reception location
❑ Decorations	❑ Decorations
❑ Food and drink	❑ Food and drink
❑ Entertainment	❑ Entertainment
❑ Attire	❑ Attire
❑ Memorabilia	❑ Memorabilia
❑ Other:	❑ Other:

∽ A P P E N D I X   B ∽

Item Estimated Cost vs. Actual Cost

You will want to create a budget up front and try to stick to it for your wedding. Use this worksheet to keep track of what you expect each aspect of your wedding to cost you. As you start to hire vendors, buy, and rent items, mark down the actual cost of each service or item. Track the difference between the estimated cost and the actual cost to determine whether you are staying within your budget or blowing your budget.

Item Estimated Cost vs. Actual Cost			
	Estimated Cost	Actual Cost	Difference
Wedding planner	$	$	$
Wedding gown	$	$	$
Wedding lingerie	$	$	$
Hair accessories	$	$	$
Wedding shoes	$	$	$
Accessories	$	$	$
Hair	$	$	$
Hairdresser gratuity	$	$	$
Makeup	$	$	$
Makeup gratuity	$	$	$

Item Estimated Cost vs. Actual Cost			
	Estimated Cost	Actual Cost	Difference
Groom's attire	$	$	$
Groom's shoes	$	$	$
Ceremony site fee	$	$	$
Officiant fee	$	$	$
Officiant gratuity	$	$	$
Ceremony programs	$	$	$
Religious items	$	$	$
Ceremony decorations	$	$	$
Ceremony musicians	$	$	$
Chair rental	$	$	$
Vehicle rental	$	$	$
Driver gratuity	$	$	$
Other ceremony expenses	$	$	$
Groom's wedding ring	$	$	$
Bride's wedding ring	$	$	$
Reception site fee	$	$	$
Catering	$	$	$
Caterer's gratuity	$	$	$
Server's gratuity	$	$	$
Liquor costs	$	$	$
Bartender gratuity	$	$	$
Wedding cake	$	$	$
Cake topper	$	$	$

Item Estimated Cost vs. Actual Cost			
	Estimated Cost	Actual Cost	Difference
Groom's cake	$	$	$
Reception decorations	$	$	$
Reception musicians	$	$	$
Musician gratuity	$	$	$
Chair/table rental	$	$	$
Dance floor rental	$	$	$
Guest book	$	$	$
Toasting glasses	$	$	$
Cake knife/server	$	$	$
Tent rental	$	$	$
Valet parking	$	$	$
Valet gratuity	$	$	$
Coat check gratuity	$	$	$
Bridal bouquet	$	$	$
Bridal party bouquets	$	$	$
Flower girl flowers	$	$	$
Ring bearer pillow	$	$	$
Mother/grandmother corsages	$	$	$
Bridal party boutonnieres	$	$	$
Father/grandfather boutonnieres	$	$	$
Other flowers	$	$	$
Photographer	$	$	$
Videographer	$	$	$

Item Estimated Cost vs. Actual Cost	Estimated Cost	Actual Cost	Difference
Save-the-date cards	$	$	$
Wedding invitations	$	$	$
Postage	$	$	$
Calligrapher	$	$	$
Thank-you cards	$	$	$
Personalized napkins/matchbooks	$	$	$
Wedding favors	$	$	$
Wedding insurance	$	$	$
Bridesmaids luncheon	$	$	$
Bridal party gifts	$	$	$
Parents' gifts	$	$	$
Rehearsal expenses	$	$	$
Rehearsal dinner	$	$	$
Honeymoon	$	$	$
Honeymoon insurance	$	$	$
Other expenses	$	$	$
Grand Total	$	$	$

Bridal Party Contact Sheet

Use this contact sheet so that you and anyone else that needs it will have all of the bridal party's contact information in one place. Rather than scramble for individual contact information, you will have a one-stop sheet with all of the information in one place.

Bridal Party Contact Sheet

Females
Role: ❑ Maid of honor ❑ Bridesmaid ❑ Flower girl
Name: _____
Address: _____
Telephone: _____ Cell phone: _____
Email address: _____
Role: ❑ Maid of honor ❑ Bridesmaid ❑ Flower girl
Name: _____
Address: _____
Telephone: _____ Cell phone: _____
Email address: _____

Role: ❏ Maid of honor ❏ Bridesmaid ❏ Flower girl

Name: _____

Address: _____

Telephone: _____ Cell phone: _____

Email address: _____

Role: ❏ Maid of honor ❏ Bridesmaid ❏ Flower girl

Name: _____

Address: _____

Telephone: _____ Cell phone: _____

Email address: _____

Role: ❏ Maid of honor ❏ Bridesmaid ❏ Flower girl

Name: _____

Address: _____

Telephone: _____ Cell phone: _____

Email address: _____

Role: ❏ Maid of honor ❏ Bridesmaid ❏ Flower girl

Name: _____

Address: _____

Telephone: _____ Cell phone: _____

Email address: _____

Role: ❏ Maid of honor   ❏ Bridesmaid   ❏ Flower girl

Name: _____

Address: _____

Telephone: _____   Cell phone: _____

Email address: _____

Role: ❏ Maid of honor   ❏ Bridesmaid   ❏ Flower girl

Name: _____

Address: _____

Telephone: _____   Cell phone: _____

Email address: _____

Males

Role: ❏ Best man   ❏ Groomsman   ❏ Usher   ❏ Ring bearer

Name: _____

Address: _____

Telephone: _____   Cell phone: _____

Email address: _____

Role: ❏ Best man   ❏ Groomsman   ❏ Usher   ❏ Ring bearer

Name: _____

Address: _____

Telephone: _____   Cell phone: _____

Email address: _____

Role: ❏ Best man ❏ Groomsman ❏ Usher ❏ Ring bearer

Name: _____

Address: _____

Telephone: _____ Cell phone: _____

Email address: _____

Role: ❏ Best man ❏ Groomsman ❏ Usher ❏ Ring bearer

Name: _____

Address: _____

Telephone: _____ Cell phone: _____

Email address: _____

Bride's Parents

Mother of the bride

Name: _____

Address: _____

Telephone: _____ Cell phone: _____

Email address: _____

Father of the bride

Name: _____

Address: _____

Telephone: _____ Cell phone: _____

Email address: _____

Groom's Parents

Mother of the groom

Name: _____

Address: _____

Telephone: _____ Cell phone: _____

Email address: _____

Father of the groom

Name: _____

Address: _____

Telephone: _____ Cell phone: _____

Email address: _____

~ A P P E N D I X   D ~

Venue Checklist for Wedding Ceremony Location

As you visit each potential venue, use this checklist as a way to keep track of the venue information. It will help you keep track of the information so that later when you review it, you can quickly narrow down which venue options fit your needs and wants and which ones do not.

Wedding Ceremony

Venue Name:	
❏ Number of guests the venue will hold	
❏ Available on your wedding date	
❏ Times available for your wedding ceremony to begin	
❏ Venue fee or donation	

Fee Includes:	
❏ Chairs/seating	
❏ Officiant/priest/preacher/minister	
❏ Parking	
❏ Decorations	
❏ Unity candle, unity candle holder, taper candles	
❏ Miscellaneous items included as part of the fee:	

	Items that I will need to rent or buy for the ceremony:	
❑		
❑		
❑		
❑		
❑		

Wedding Reception Venue Checklist

Venue Name: _____

❑	Number of guests that the venue will hold		
❑	Available on your wedding date		
❑	Times available on Your wedding date		
❑	Venue fee		
❑	In-house caterer	❑	Need to hire my own caterer
❑	Tables	❑	Chairs (specialty or banquet)
❑	Chair covers	Color choices:	
❑	Table covers	Color choices:	
❑	Linen napkins	Color choices:	
❑	Plates, bowls, cups, flatware, etc. provided?		
❑	Wait staff provided	How many per # of guests?	
❑	Bartender(s) provided	How many per # of guests?	
❑	Dance floor	How many people does it hold?	
❑	If ceremony and/or reception is to be held outside, where is the backup location in case of bad weather?		
❑	How many other events will be held at the same time as your wedding?		
❑	Will you have dedicated staff for your event?		

Optional services or products that the venue offers:	
❑	
❑	
❑	
❑	
❑	
❑	
❑	
❑	
❑	
❑	

Wedding Invitations & Wedding Stationery Checklist

When you place your invitation and wedding stationery order, use this checklist to make sure you do not forget anything.

❑	Save-the-date cards	
❑	Wedding invitations	
❑	Reception cards	
❑	Response cards	
❑	Thank-you cards	
❑	Envelope addressing	
❑	Reception seating place cards/seating chart	
❑	Postage (invitations & response cards)	
❑	Wedding programs	
❑	Map/directions (From ceremony to reception)	
❑	Miscellaneous costs	

～ A P P E N D I X   F ～

Flower Checklist

When you place your flower order, use this checklist to make sure you do not forget anything.

❏	Bride bouquet	
❏	Toss bouquet	
❏	Bride flowers for hair or veil	
❏	Maid-of-honor bouquet	
❏	Matron-of-honor bouquet	
❏	Bridesmaid bouquets	
❏	Flowers for bridesmaids' hair	
❏	Flower girl bouquet/flower petals for flower basket	
❏	Flower girl flowers for hair	
❏	Groom boutonniere	
❏	Best man boutonniere	
❏	Usher boutonnieres	
❏	Ring Bearer boutonniere	
❏	Groomsmen boutonnieres	
❏	Mother of the bride hand bouquet or corsage	
❏	Mother of the groom hand bouquet or corsage	
❏	Father of the bride boutonniere	
❏	Father of the groom boutonniere	
❏	Grandmother flowers	
❏	Grandfather boutonnieres	

Ceremony flowers	
❏ Entrance or archway flowers	
❏ Altar arrangements	
❏ Chuppah (for Jewish ceremonies)	
❏ Pew flowers/decorations	
❏ Chair flowers/decorations	

Reception flowers	
❏ Table centerpieces	
❏ Buffet/food tables	
❏ Bride & groom table (sweetheart table)	
❏ Head table (For bridal party)	
❏ Place card table/seating chart easel	
❏ Cake and/or cake table	
❏ Bathrooms	
❏ Entrance way	
❏ Guest book table	
❏ Gift table	
❏ Place card table	
❏ Bar	

~ A P P E N D I X   G ~

Wedding Ceremony Music

Provide this song list to your wedding DJ or live band so they know what music to play and when to play it.

Songs to play while guests are being seated:	

Song for the seating of the mothers:

Song for the bridal party (procession):

Song for the bride:

If you choose, songs can also be performed or played at different points during the ceremony. You will need to talk about this with the person performing your ceremony when you are discussing the actual ceremony order including vows, readings, and music.

Song(s) for during the ceremony:	
Song for the recession (others, fathers and bridal party to exit):	
Song for the bride & groom to exit:	
Song to play while your guests exit:	
Miscellaneous songs:	

Reception Music

Background music for your guests during cocktail hour:	

Songs to play while guests Are seated for the reception:	

Song for introduction of the wedding party:	

Order that the wedding party should be announced:	
Bridesmaid	Groomsmen
Maid of honor:	Best man:
Flower girl:	Ring bearer:

Song for the announcement of the bride & groom:

Bride & groom's first dance:

Bride & father dance:

Groom & mother dance:

Songs for the dinner hour:	

Song for the bouquet toss:

Song for the garter toss:

Song for cake-cutting ceremony:

Songs for dancing & partying After dinner:	

Last dance song:

Bride & groom exit song:

Photographs and Video

Use this sheet to work with your photographer and videographer. Provide the checklist to each professional so they know the "must obtain" shots and those that you would like to have but are not as crucial for you.

Traditional formal photos	
❏ Bride and groom	
❏ Bride with her mother	
❏ Bride with her father	
❏ Bride with her parents	
❏ Bride with groom's parents	
❏ Groom with his mother	
❏ Groom with his father	
❏ Groom with his parents	
❏ Groom with bride's parents	
❏ Bride with bridesmaids	
❏ Groom with groomsmen	
❏ Entire wedding party	
❏ Bride and groom with grandparents, godparents, and other relatives	

Candid photos	
❏ Bride getting ready	
❏ Bride and attendants	
❏ Groom getting ready	

❑	Groom with groomsmen	
❑	Bride walking down the aisle father	
❑	Attendants coming down the aisle	
❑	Bride's mother walking down the aisle	
❑	Groom's parents walking down the aisle	
❑	Bride being "given away" at by father	
❑	Wedding party at the altar	
❑	Exchange of vows	
❑	Exchange of the rings	
❑	The kiss	
❑	Both sets of parents walking back down the aisle during the recession	
❑	Bridal party walking back down the aisle (recession)	
❑	Ring bearer and flower girl walking back down the aisle (recession)	
❑	Bride and groom recessing	

Reception photos		
❑	Room setup	
❑	Bridal party table and/or bride and groom table	
❑	Food/buffet table	
❑	Cake table	
❑	Gift table	
❑	Place card table/seating chart easel	
❑	Bride & groom arriving at the reception	
❑	Bridal party introductions	
❑	Bride and groom introduction	
❑	Bride and groom's first dance	
❑	Bride and father dance	
❑	Groom and mother dance	

❏	Cake-cutting ceremony	
❏	Father of the bride toast	
❏	Best man's toast	
❏	Bride and groom toasting each other	
❏	Garter toss	
❏	Bouquet toss	
❏	Placing of the garter on recipient of bouquet	
❏	Guest dancing	
❏	Guests seated at the tables	
❏	Guests partying and having fun	
❏	Bride and groom leaving the reception	

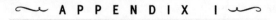

~ A P P E N D I X 1 ~

Attire

As you are checking your list to make sure you everything you need to dress for the part on your wedding day, use this checklist as your guide.

Bride:		
❑ Wedding dress/gown		
❑ Bra/underwear		
❑ Shoes		
❑ Garter		
❑ Jewelry		
❑ Veil/headpiece		
❑ Panty hose/stockings		
❑ Slip		

Groom:		
❑ Shirt		
❑ Tie		
❑ Vest/cummerbund		
❑ Pants		
❑ Tux or suit jacket		
❑ Socks		
❑ Shoes		

Author Bio

Copywriter and marketing consultant Kristie Lorette is passionate about helping entrepreneurs and businesses create copy and marketing pieces that sizzle, motivate, and sell. It is through her more than 14 years of experience working in various roles of marketing, including running an event and wedding planning service of her own for four years, that Lorette developed her widespread expertise in advanced business, marketing strategies, and communications. Lorette earned her  B.S. in marketing and B.S. in multinational business from Florida State University, and her M.B.A. from Nova Southeastern University.

Index